Linda Cracknell was born in 1959 in the Netherlands. She grew up in Surrey and studied English and Fine Art at Exeter University. She went on to complete a Postgraduate Certificate in Education at the Institute of Education, London. For the past ten years Linda has lived and worked in Scotland. She lives in Perthshire where she works for the WWF – the global environment network. Linda was winner of the *Macallan/Scotland on Sunday* short story competition in 1998 with *Life Drawing*, her first published work. Since then she has had five further short stories published. Short stories by Linda have also been broadcast on BBC Radio 4.

Life Drawing

www.11-9.co.uk

Life Drawing
Linda Cracknell

First published by

303a The Pentagon Centre
36 Washington Street
GLASGOW
G3 8AZ
Tel: 0141-204-1109
Fax: 0141-221-5363
E-mail: info@nwp.sol.co.uk
http://www.11-9.co.uk

A catalogue record for this
book is available from the
British Library.

11:9 is funded by the Scottish Arts
Council National Lottery Fund.

ISBN 1-903238-13-7

Typeset in Utopia
Designed by Mark Blackadder

Printed by WS Bookwell, Finland

In memory of Hugh

Acknowledgements

I would like to thank Sara Maitland for guidance and encouragement in various capacities and the Open College of the Arts for the stimulus provided by their creative writing courses whilst writing many of these stories.

Thanks go to previous publishers of the following stories in this collection:

Life Drawing was first published in Polygon's *Shorts* anthology (The Macallan/Scotland on Sunday Short Story Collection). It also appeared in *Scotland on Sunday* and was broadcast on Radio Scotland's *Storyline* in August 1998.

The Fall was broadcast on Radio Four's *Late Book* in January 1999 and was published in *The Keekin-Gless*, an anthology from Perth and Kinross Libraries in April 1999.

Mother's Boy was published in Polygon's *Shorts 2* anthology *(The Macallan/Scotland on Sunday Short Story Collection)* in August 1999.

Death Wish was published in *Something Wicked*, New Scottish Crime Writing from Polygon, in October 1999.

Keeping Away from the Water was published in *Product* magazine in February 2000.

Holiday Money was published in *Chapman* magazine, issue 96, June 2000.

I would also like to thank the following for the use of an extract from:

Moondance
Words and Music by Van Morrison
© 1970 Caledonia Soul Music/Warner-Tamerlane Publishing Corp, USA
Warner/Chappell Music Ltd, London W6 8BS
Lyric reproduced by permission of:
IMP Ltd, London W6 8BS

Contents

Mother's Boy

I'm waiting for Mum, like I do every night. Ben's cheek squashes pink onto the pillow next to me. Mr Brock's paw is in his mouth. His breath gurgles a bit as he sleeps. The stove hums and smoke crackles up the chimney in the middle of the bender, our home. Dad's on his bed. His cigarette smoke wafts over to me and I hear the flick of his magazine pages, the creak of the mattress as he fidgets, reaching up to the hammock above his bed to pull things down. Books or clothes. His candlelight makes the bender brighter than it is by day. If I look carefully, I can see the frame which Dad made by bending tree branches. They're a bit hidden now by all the cloths and blankets stuffed behind them. Dad said the blankets were to make it warmer – warmer than it would be with just the tarpaulin over us, or the Tarp as we call it. I make it into a game, passing lots of time while Mum's not there by searching for branches among the dark folds.

Once Dad's put his candle out, there's no difference whether my eyes are open or closed. But I don't need eyes. I lie and listen to all the cars going by on the main road to the town. It depends on which way the wind's blowing as to how clear they are. If it's raining, they sizzle like eggs frying on our stove. I always know when it's her coming. I know the exact signs. The way the car slows down to turn into the track. At first you just hear the bumps and sucks of the puddles as she makes her way towards us, climbing towards our camping place. Then the engine sound grows, and finally, once she's passed the bend, Mum's Lights shine in through our only window – the one made out of see-through plastic. They cast a square of light onto the wall. It's criss-crossed, like the light from an old-fashioned lantern on a Christmas card. As she nears us, the square of light squashes and gets long. It moves up the wall, slides and curves along the whole tunnel of the ceiling.

Then Mum's Lights hit the mirror. White, and getting larger.

Dad always goes to sleep before Mum comes home. And then I wait for her on my own. She works in a factory making sweeties – toffees and fudge. She calls the factory the 'Stink Tank'. To make sweeties she puts all the things like sugar and butter into this huge tank a bit like a swimming pool and they get mixed up. You smell her when she comes home. I guess it's because bits splash up when she's leaning over to stir it. It's a heavy, sweet smell that lands on you after she's walked past in the dark. I don't mind it but I think Dad does.

Dad found the mirror in a skip, said its owners didn't want it but it would do for us. Mum looked into it and screwed up her face, said she looked so old these days, that was what working nights did to you. She didn't want it. I put it at the bottom of my bed. So although as I lie there I face away from the window, I can see the reflection of Mum's Lights. She bounces home towards me. The lights put warmth into my tummy. I can go to sleep.

After the lights have slipped off the edge of the mirror, the car stops and the engine clicks off. Sometimes she doesn't come in straight away – says she likes to have a cigarette out there in the dark rather than disturbing us. And I'm usually falling asleep by the time I hear the car door slam and the flap of the Tarp as she comes in the porch. She always whispers Hi to Taff. Taff's old bones click as he wakes a bit and stretches his legs. His tail beats on the floor. Mum says it's the sheepdog in him, not happy until he has his whole flock together. Then the smoke shoots up my nostrils as she puts another log on the stove.

If she crackles when she comes in, it means she's brought us a bag of toffees. Rejects, she calls them. They taste all right, though sometimes the wrappers are more on the inside than the outside. She never eats them herself. And she pushes me away if I eat them too close to her, says the smell makes her feel sick. She doesn't want to be reminded of the Stink Tank when she's at home. One day me and Ben went to Jason Clark's house after school. We took a big bag of Rejects and we watched *Grange Hill*. When Mum came to collect us, she said she was calling us from the doorway for five minutes before we noticed her. We were staring at the TV, with toffee wrappers a mile high around us and our faces all brown. Later on Ben was sick. She didn't bring Rejects home for a while after that.

Then you hear her pull the covers back to get into bed and a few sleepy whispers with Dad as she settles next to him. Their voices are usually too soft to hear the words. But there was one time, a few weeks ago, when I heard what they were saying.

—You turning your back on me? Mum said.

Some mumbles buzzed between them, getting louder like wasps when you try and swat them. Dad did his Giant's Voice.

—You smell like a fucking crème caramel.

—All part of a night's work. One of us has to earn some money round here you know. There was a sharp creak of movement. I could picture her glaring at where his face should be in the dark.

—Yes, sweetness. There was a pause and then the snap of his jaw as he finished a yawn. I'm just not in the mood for sticky toffee pudding at four am.

—You … Jesus! The smell's not my fault. Some of us aren't on 'hot bath' terms with the local tarts.

I hadn't heard her yelp like that before. I do it when I get really cross with Ben and want to hit him but know I mustn't. But not Mum.

Dad laughed, and not long afterwards Mum jostled down as his snores started again. I didn't get to sleep for a while after that. Mum was sniffing.

• • • • • • • • • • • • • • • • • •

While I wait, I use the heavy black torch and Dad says not to waste the batteries. In the dark I hold it against my hands and feet. They go dark pink. I can see these red stick things inside, like a skeleton except different. I'm transparent. I don't know any other boys at school who are. Like some sort of alien. I don't think Mum knows, although she realizes I'm a bit special. What would we all do without you Jack, she said, when they were both in bed with flu and I had to keep the stove going and walk to the shop to buy food.

It must have been boring before I had the mirror. Every night now there's a boy called James who appears in it. We speak to each other in whispers so we don't wake the others. He tells me about things that no one at school knows anything about. And I don't tell anyone, not even Mum or Dad or Ben. It's our secret. I only need the torch and the mirror to make him appear. I sit in bed and shine the torch upwards from the blankets under my chin.

James says that if I concentrate hard enough, I can become anything. Like a bird, or like Robert Chatham, so I can do brilliant cartwheels. Or I could turn into a warrior and be able to beat up the big boys who say 'Crusty' at me and call Ben 'Smoky Bacon' which makes him cry. They find it funny that our clothes smell of smoke. It's just because Mum hangs them to dry on a rack above the stove. She says that was why she cut all Ben's hair off before he started school – so he wouldn't get called names. I'm not sure why she's never done that for me. She thinks I can look after myself I suppose. It didn't work for Ben anyway. They still call him names.

Sometimes I hear voices while I wait. Outside. The first time I thought it was like a whole playground of children chattering and squawking. But more beautiful. Like a playground would sound in heaven. I went outside to see what was happening. But there was nothing. There was just trees and a light sky which confused me because I thought it was night. The bender looked so small and low huddled against the wall of the ruined house for shelter. And Mum wasn't back yet. Then Dad came out to find me, said I was a pillock. It was birds. Birds. Where are they then? I asked. He said they were in the trees, go back to bed. But I had to keep asking. Why are they making so much noise, they don't sound like that during the day? He said they're just happy to be alive, which you won't be unless you get back in there fast.

Dad spent a few nights away from home around that time. Mum watched him walk off down the track. The metal buckles on his rucksack glinted off the full moon. Bloody werewolf, I heard her say at his shadow.

It was later that night I went to look for aliens. James told me that alien landings always happen at full moons. And they'd be sure to land on the hill up behind the bender. I was going to go on my own but Mum was looking a bit sad so I asked her to come too.

I walked a bit ahead of Mum. The aliens would need to see me first; they'd recognize me. I carried the big torch but I kept it turned off. Each time I looked back, I could see Mum's outline following, a tall shadow with her head bent and long hair swinging out from her shoulders. Taff ran ahead.

After I'd climbed the gate, and I was under the big oak trees, it was dead dark. I followed the rustle of Taff upwards on a kind of path I knew was there in daylight. His paws stopped and pee crackled against fallen branches. Otherwise my breath was the only thing I could sense; it formed clouds in front of my face and came out in big puffs from the climb. Looking back over my shoulder there were tree trunks and the gate patterned against the town's orange lights, and Mum climbing over the gate towards me from the moonlit field. The black shape of hills rose beyond the town. I turned upwards. Branches brushed the top of my hat and something reached up to lick at my legs. I'd lost the path. I tripped on a root and went face down. My hands were wet, and a fungus smell went up my nose. I put on the torch so I could see better. But the opposite happened. Everything disappeared, and when I looked back – no

Mum. I flashed the torch below me but she wasn't there. I started calling her. Then I was stumbling back down the hill until the panting filled up my ears. I heard nothing, saw nothing, until I ran right into her. And her arms wrapped me. And Taff was jumping up at us thinking it was a game.

She laughed and said, You came back to find your poor lost Mum, hey?

We walked back down to the bender; me lighting the way with the torch and her with her arm around me, saying I was her big brave boy.

• • • • • • • • • • • • • • • • •

One night last week I heard those high voices again. They went on for ever. And then I saw not Mum's Lights but the sun, coming out properly and reflecting in the mirror at the bottom of the bed. I hadn't heard the car. And then Dad was out of bed, his vest and trousers on, stooping out of the porch without saying anything to me or Ben. I heard him chopping wood with the axe. With every chop there was another noise – like the noise the dog made when I saw it get run over on the main road. Taff, I thought. What's he doing to Taff? But when I got outside, Taff was lying there as usual and he looked up at me like he wanted me to explain something, his stomach stuck to the ground. He looked back at Dad, one ear crooked. It was daylight and the car wasn't there. Then I realized that it was Dad making the noise. Every time the axe came down the noise came out of him. When he turned towards me and Taff, his face was all ugly and looked wet. Where's Mum I said, but he looked away and said something about visiting a friend and stared hard at the log before he split it. And Ben and me went to school but we forgot our reading books, and we were still wondering where she was. I told Ben that she'd gone to have her cigarette somewhere else so she wouldn't wake us.

After school she was there as usual to meet us.

• • • • • • • • • • • • • • • • •

Here she comes. The car's bumping along the track. The headlights start to do their thing on our ceiling. I say bye to James, switch the torch off and lie back, watch Mum's Lights bouncing towards home. The handbrake cranks on outside and I settle down to sleep.

The flap of the Tarp jolts me back awake. Something's different. The engine's still futting in the dark outside. She's forgotten to turn it off. I clamp my eyes shut as I always do, to look like I've been asleep for hours. Taff clicks and grunts but she doesn't speak to him. The footsteps creep up to our bed, and I feel Ben's side of the mattress bounce upwards. She's carrying him somewhere, all sleep-heavy. I squint through lash fringes and see her legs by the side of the bed, Mr Brock black and white on an empty pillow. The Stink Tank smell gets stronger and I can almost feel her warm fudge chocolate breath on my cheek. I know she's bending over me. But I'm asleep Mum, just like I always am when you come home. You never need to worry about me.

Then her legs through the fringes move away and I hold my breath. Frozen in pretend sleep. Straining to listen. Flap. She's back outside. A car door squeaks and slams. Ben first of course, the Baby of the Family. Then she'll come back for me. I wait. I hear another car door shut. The engine roars, the wheels slip on mud. She's going. Then the engine stops. My breath gushes out.

But there's no 'flap' of her coming back for me. The engine re-starts with a cough. Mud splatters off the tyres against the Tarp. Then the car's getting quieter as it leaves us, away down the track. I open my eyes properly. No need to pretend now. In the mirror Mum's Lights are bouncing. But they're red and they're getting smaller, closer together. They disappear into the dark around the bend and I can only just hear the engine. The car stops at the end of the track, pulls away down the main road. And then it's quiet and dark.

Reflections

Three barefoot carpet steps across the bedroom and Julie was at the mirror again. Book in hand, she raised her chin for a meeting of eyes in the glass.

Give me my robe, put on my crown;
I have immortal longings in me.

Her voice sounded squeaky and thin rather than low and sexy as she imagined Cleopatra's would. Her face in the mirror was too girlish and spotty. She was missing gold earrings, dark ringlets around her face, black-lined eyes. She toyed for a moment with the make-up on a shelf below the mirror – mascara, eyeliner, lipstick. But there was no point. Tragedy didn't show in her face, and no handmaids would come running to dress her.

She saw the room behind her in the mirror. Framing it this way made her look at it more carefully than normal. She saw a clutter of shapes – revision books spread across the bed, a teddy bear coming up for air among the heap of knotted clothes. A banana settled blackly on the dressing table next to a bottle of pore cleanser, a screwed up chocolate wrapper and four empty coffee cups. Perhaps this was why her dragon-mother loved her so much. Why she was an outcast from the family.

She fingered the slippery fabric of the new purple dress, still un-worn, draped over the corner of the mirror. Long and slim with bootlace straps and a logo on the front, she was saving it for the end-of-school dance. She'd surprise everyone. She was going to pluck her eyebrows pencil-thin and put kohl around her lashes like she'd seen in magazines. She'd be sleek as a serpent.

She spoke again to the face in front of her.

Sometimes we see a cloud that's dragonish;
A vapour sometime like a bear or rock,
A forked mountain, or blue promontory
With trees upon't that nod unto the world

And ... something ... *our eyes with air.*

She searched at the open book. 'Mock. That's it ... *mock our eyes with air.'*

The words were getting jumbled. Just like the confusion of clouds and dragons, Act Three, Scene Two was getting muddled with Act Five, Scene Three. Asps, barges and tripartite heroes got whisked together in her mind, like egg yolks in a mixing bowl losing their distinctness, becoming one runny mess. And what did it mean anyway, *mock our eyes with air?*

The mirror mocked her too. Mocked her desire to be cool like Cleopatra – with looks to stun everyone at countless parties, and lots of jewellery to dangle. It merely showed a schoolgirl incarcerated in her bedroom for the last seventeen years, allowed out only for English Literature exams. 'Really Julie, what an imagination. You do exaggerate,' her mother had said a couple of days ago when she came off the phone to a friend, explaining how she couldn't get out to buy a pair of shoes before the school dance. 'What?' she glared at her mother. 'You shouldn't listen in to private conversations you know.' She knew very well how far the leash really stretched – to the boundaries of her bedroom.

As a small child she was fascinated by the invisible trail which followed her mother. Perfume. It wafted in the air as she passed, clung to clothes, even scented the plates they ate off. You could always tell where she'd been. Julie used to follow the trail to her mother's bedroom door. She stood mesmerized, watching the slim back at the dressing table. She saw in the reflection the flouncing movements of her mother's wrists, the swan-like thrust of her chin towards the mirror as she squirted her neck from a big glass bottle. Julie's concentration gave her presence away in the end. Her mother swivelled around when she heard the long breaths. On one occasion she was chased out, the door banged shut, her mother saying she'd 'had enough'. When her mother was hanging the washing in the garden later, Julie trespassed back into the bedroom to try the dressing-table rites herself. She slipped ankle-socked feet into high heels and dragged a red line across her face, breaking off the tip of the gold-cased lipstick. The screams brought her mother running when she showered perfume into her eyes, her aim confused by the mirror.

Julie had no idea if her mother still used perfume. She wasn't aware of smelling it anymore.

Revising. Boring. Bored.

Why was she learning stupid phrases off by heart? As if they were going to be of any use to her in a few weeks' time when she was free of school and sitting behind a Tesco till for the summer. That's forty-three pounds, madam, and can I interest you in a recitation of the barge speech? For a fifty pence special offer I can give you a glimpse of a throne burning on the water and summon lovesick winds. Today only though, madam.

She'd have to pass the time reflecting on her own tragedy instead, wondering whether she would be going to a university in another city, where she would know no one and be left talking to another mirror, no better off than she was now. At least it would relieve her parents. She imagined her mother, protected by a scaly, heat-resistant suit, torching her room clear once she was out the way.

Downstairs, in the out-of-bounds-to-revising-teenagers lounge, the TV shrieked studio laughter, echoed by her Mum and Dad in chorus. She looked at her watch. Eight-thirty pm. Only twelve hours and thirty minutes until the last exam; the only obstacle between her and freedom. But her brains were like spaghetti. How was she ever going to remember all this stuff?

She shuffled back to the bed and fell board-like onto her back. Something pressed between her shoulder blades, and she reached back to pull out a bent book and her teddy bear.

'Hi Ted, how're you doing?' She held him above her on straight arms so they were eye to eye, animated him with small jerks.

Sometime like a bear, a rock, a forked fountain.
Hell, wasn't it 'mountain'? She dropped Ted and scrabbled for the book to check. Then she dropped the book and picked up Ted again. Perhaps he would bring her better luck, sitting on the desk in front of her in the exam, than the photo of the lush Leonardo? But he was uncool. He should go to a jumble sale. After tomorrow she was for the big world, not this place. She opened her arms to embrace the small room and all its childish mess. What would she want with a teddy? She was going to be an Egyptian princess and take baths with perfumed oils.

She refused to think of Ted's fur wet with sobs, and the way she'd gripped his spongy body half to death on several nights recently. She lifted him by an ear and tossed him at the wall. He thudded against her Robbie poster and then flopped onto the pile of dirty clothes below. He was caught mid-cartwheel, his head buried in the clothes, the worn pads of one back paw stretching towards the ceiling.

She looked at her watch again. Panic began to contract her belly. She knew nothing. Had forgotten everything. And now she was wasting time. It was as if a revision burglar had sneaked into her mind and filled his swag bag with all the iambic pentameters and rhyming couplets she'd been learning by heart the last few weeks.

Concentrate.

She heard laughter flutter around the downstairs of the house again. Heard her Dad call 'Tea or coffee?' through from the kitchen to the lounge. 'Yeah, tea, Dad, please,' she said to herself, knowing the offer wasn't coming. Then she screamed at the top of her voice, *'Give me to drink mandragora.'* No response. Maybe Dad didn't know where to find the mandragora in the kitchen cupboards.

She could manage the whole drink-making thing without having to speak to them if she timed it right. During *Eastenders* she didn't need to fear the click of steps across the tiled hall, the creature coming on clawed feet to breathe fire at her for making a mess in the kitchen, for being out of her room, for being *her*. No, her mother wouldn't leave the TV for anything.

The Walkman was protection too. She put it on to move around the house. 'Like living with a deaf-mute,' her Dad said. One evening she'd put the Walkman down in the kitchen while she made a phone call. She had to rip it off her Dad's head when she got off the phone. 'A bit up to date for you I think, Dad.' And he'd glared after her from the bottom of the stairs as she stomped back to her refuge. 'A bit tuneless, more like.'

Back to the book. She scanned the page, then scowled at the wall opposite.

... Other women cloy the appetites they feed.
She looked down to find the next lines.

But she makes hungry where most she satisfies.
She caught the hint of a smirk coming from the banana on the dressing table. She tried to ignore it. *'Other women cloy ...'* It was sick – the suggestion she should bite into its flesh, when it had been sitting there rotting for weeks, like a yellow and black slug. She resisted the urge to slap it into a pulp and picked it up by its blackened stalk. It seemed to throb slightly against her hand as if it were laughing. She pulled back the curtain, stood on the bed, opened the small top window, and flung the banana into the front garden. She watched with satisfaction as it burst on the gravel.

As she climbed back down from the bed, her hand crunched on a pile of sun-dried flies which had been collecting on the windowsill during her incarceration. It made her look down and notice the pebble that she kept there, ground flat and smooth by waves on a Cornish beach. She held it in the palm of her hand and looked at it first one way up and then the other way. Where was the face in it – the reason that she'd chosen it all those years ago? She didn't seem to be able to find the quartz eyes and mouth that had once seemed so obvious against the granite.

She returned to the mirror, but it disappointed again – still no resemblance to Cleopatra. She picked up the eye-liner and drew a bold feline shape around one eye, turning the line upwards almost to meet the eyebrow at the outside edge. Cool. But the open book on the bed summoned her back before she could have a good look.

Concentrate.

Get on with it.

Not long to go.

At this rate she wasn't even going to get through the exam. Afterwards there'd be one more day in school to get the class photo taken, have a drink with the teachers, and wave goodbye. Would her mother look up from the TV for long enough to notice that she was launching herself into the world?

It had been different for her big sister's exams. Things changed in the family. Chocolate biscuits appeared in the cupboards and came out on plates for Fiona's scheduled breaks. Her mother had insisted on a half hour for every two hours of study. A revision timetable was pinned to the kitchen wall. There were whispers about the need for Fiona to relax; she was working too hard.

There was a sunny Sunday in the middle of Fiona's exams when her mother packed a picnic into an old basket and put on a floral dress. They went out as a family and ate scotch eggs and strawberries on a riverbank. Even now it remained a vivid picture. There was a sense of special occasion which Julie associated with violets. She remembered running along the edges of the meadow, where the trees stooped over it, stopping to touch the purple jewels which illuminated the bank. She called out as she found each new cluster. The violets stretched up, smoothing open all their folds and intricacies like naked sunbathers. The other three sat on a blanket, chatting. Julie pictured her mother on that blanket. Her legs were curled to one side, the thin dress fabric revealing the line of her sharp spine. She leant towards Fiona like she was crouching over guarded treasure.

She realized that her hand was at her hair, and

found a smooth patch on the crown of her head. The mirror confirmed it – a little bald lump of pink. One day, sitting downstairs with her Walkman on, she'd seen her Dad pull a 'zombie' face and mimic a monkey picking at the top of its head. Her mother had laughed. Julie didn't realize when she was doing it. A few days ago she'd found clumps of hair in her hand when she looked up from exam papers as the invigilator called time.

She needed action. She picked through her make-up, slashed vamp red across her lips, dusted blusher onto her cheeks, completed the second cat's eye. She pushed her chin up, towards the mirror, Walkman on. Then she noticed something cruel in her reflection. How dare it. She would never look like her mother. Not even when she was ancient and forty years old. She pouted, super-model style, to remove the image, pulled the new purple dress from the corner of the mirror, and flourished it in front of her.

Julie hadn't worn it yet, but she had a sense from the mirror that another body had been inside the dress. It looked as though there were dents in the stretchy fabric. Dents that had been made by boobs. There was only one possible culprit; her mother. Her mother, whom she thought never came into the room. She obviously hadn't been coming in for housework – never did, judging by the plague pit of dead flies. But perhaps she snooped about when Julie was doing exams; hunting for her diary, sniffing for drugs or hidden contraceptives; looking for something to give her a hard time about.

Or maybe, just maybe, her mother was sad enough to try on Julie's clothes, use her make-up, even. Who knows, maybe she'd been trying to look like Cleopatra too? After all, she had asked to see the book the other day, and lingered over the pages of Elizabeth Taylor in that Egyptian gear.

Julie turned away from the mirror and stood in the centre of the room. She didn't need to move, felt she could practically touch each wall by spinning slowly in its centre with her arms outstretched. She knew the inside of every drawer and cupboard, what was under the bed. Even the shape of the cobwebs around the light shade. It was her room. Her lonely room. She never thought of someone else knowing it, her mother knowing it, wanting to know it.

She focused on the face in the mirror. A painted schoolgirl. Behind it she saw the door swing open. Her mother's head appeared.

'All right love? Don't stay up too late. Remember you need to be fresh for the morning.'

Julie heard it remotely through the Walkman, but she didn't answer.

Framed in the mirror, the head remained protruding into the room, like a turtle. 'I'll wake you at seven.'

Julie turned to look at her. She stared down at the dress to formulate her accusation. What would she say? It didn't seem to look so stretched now. Maybe she'd been mistaken, seen a dragon when she should have seen a cloud. Maybe her eyes had been 'mocked with air'.

'Ooh, you're glam. You trying out your look for the dance?' Her mother pointed at the dress. 'I've got something. To go with it. I'll get it.'

By the time her mother came back, Julie had put on the purple dress. She opened the small black box while her mother lifted her T-shirt and jeans off the floor and folded them. A single purple stone was suspended from a silver chain.

'Here.' Her mother stood behind her at the mirror, fastened the chain around Julie's neck. 'Lovely. It goes well.'

Julie saw herself in purple, with dark eyes, glittering with new jewellery, her chin thrusting upwards. She saw the face behind her. Noticed the swan-like neck. Maybe even caught a slight breath of perfume in the air that wafted between them when she turned to kiss her mother on the cheek.

'Thanks, Mum.'

'Sleep well, love.' She slipped across the room and nudged the bedroom door closed behind her.

Julie started to undress and wipe the make-up off her face. She picked Ted off the floor and put him back on the bed. She needed to go to bed, her mother was right, but overnight she might forget all the quotes she'd learnt. She picked up the book again.

Concentrate.

Just one more.

'*Unarm Eros;*' she said to the mirror. '*The long day's task is done, And we must sleep.*'

Painting the Shiver

Carl Ferry moved into Rowan Cottage in August. After the Pickford's vans had been nodded through the village, his beaten up Merc pulled up outside the Post Office. He was dressed head to toe in black, including a broad-brimmed hat. Tall, with shoulder-length grey hair, all eyes on the street clung to him, then fluttered away in a gesture of nonchalance. Alan's Mum, who worked at the Post Office, reported afterwards to anyone who wanted to know, that he bought candles, cigarette papers and a ginger cake. He'd wanted white spirit, but they didn't stock it.

August always brought new faces. Visitors. At that time of year the heather halted cars in their tracks. Cameras on legs disgorged onto the verges. They didn't bother Alan much as he didn't drive. But he was affected, like everyone in the village. It drove the locals mad; induced suicidal overtaking. 'Why can't they just be satisfied with one of these,' his Mum would say, shaking her head over the purple-next-to-the-sea postcards she tried to sell. 'Why do they all need to take their own pictures?'

When Rowan Cottage came on the market, Alan had sat through the conversations in the pub. Robert Mackinnon was convinced that his daughter and her family were going to get it; someone else had friends who wanted it for a holiday cottage; it was tied up about fifty times over. In the event, the highest bidder came from outside. All the way from Glasgow. That was the only thing which made Alan prick up his ears, as he was thinking of taking a course in Glasgow. He'd applied anyway. Something to do. A wee change from earning a pittance doing the gardens around the village. He'd think about it if they offered him a place.

A couple of weeks after he moved in, some of the boxes and crates still remained in Carl Ferry's garden. 'I hope he's going to mow the lawn,' said Alan's Mum. 'It was a beautiful garden when the Johnsons were there. Nice people. And if he doesn't move those boxes the grass'll die underneath.'

Alan passed Rowan Cottage most days, walking between the farm and the village. He was used to looking at people's gardens critically, gauging character by them. The debris that he saw in Carl Ferry's garden issued warnings about the man. There was a male mannequin, from a department store or something. It stood, toes up, heels down, propped against the side wall of the house. It only had one arm and a red heart shape was painted on its chest. A tartan scarf was tied around its hips, covering its privates. Opposite was another figure, made of stone, the sort you see in big gardens and stately homes. She had a quiver of arrows over her shoulder and carried a small bow. Why would anyone who was *not* off their head have such things in their garden? The guy was a nutter. For sure.

There were discussions in the pub about the newcomer. There had to be. There always was a flurry of interest when new people first appeared. Like earlier in the summer when a minibus of DJs from London had turned up to run a dance in the village hall. No one spoke to them directly – that wasn't the way. But their baggy trousers and flower pot hats were noted, and the way they said 'wicked' all the time. Folk went along to the dance to see what it was all about, but Malky, the factor on the local estate, had refused to hear the new sounds they were playing and jived along with one of the girls, exactly as he would have done to Bill Haley in his youth. They got in the minibus and went back to London the next day.

What else was there to talk about except Carl Ferry? Someone who worked night shifts reported seeing the lights on at three am every morning. He was rarely seen during the day. When he did leave the house, he was always dressed in black, his skin looked pallid and a cigarette hung from his lips.

'You can be sure of one thing,' said Robert

Mackinnon. 'He'll not be coming along to the community council.'

'What the hell does he *do*, anyway?'

And soon the word went up that he was an artist. It resonated like approaching thunder, announcing itself in the Post Office and then moving on to pub, breakfast table, farm gate. An artist. Unlike the London DJs, he showed no sign of going away again, and rather than dying down, the discussions escalated. Everyone was on watch. Alan had never attended the pub so religiously, enjoying each new building block that was added to the construction of Carl Ferry's character.

'Saw him up in one of my fields today. Christ knows what he was doing. He walked round in a circle.' Robert dipped a fat finger in his beer and traced it on the bar, 'Then he stopped and wrote things in a wee book.'

'You want to watch your sheep, pal,' said Tam. 'If they start disappearing, you'll know where to look. In cross-section in the Kelvin what's-is-name museum, like the woolly bugger in that gallery in London.' This even fetched a smile onto the face of Archie behind the bar. The others roared.

'And they call it effing art,' Robert's son, Willy, paused for effect, still in his wellies and overalls from a day earning good money on the fish farm. Alan had shared girlfriends, football stories and horizons with him all the way through school. Now he saw for the first time the thickening under Willy's chin that gave him the shadow-look of his dad. And he was taking on the same nightly growl over his eighty-shillings. 'You can be sure of one thing. It's us mugs that's paying for it.'

'Hey, Alan,' Robert called from the other end of the bar, 'they're not going to turn you into one of these arty-farty types at college, are they?'

'It's technical drawing I'm doing. Art's just an option, like. Anyway, don't know if I'm going yet.'

• • • • • • • • • • • • • • • • • • •

One Friday night Willy was driving Alan and another boy home from a fancy dress party at the pub. Willy mislaid the road on his way up the village street and buried the front of the car in a flower-bed. As reverse gear and his co-ordination had vaporized, they abandoned the car and continued on foot. At the crossroads, a scarecrow, a vampire and a nurse parted company and walked home in different directions.

Alan's way was illuminated by a full moon. He'd never really stopped to think about it before, but it was mysterious. Night time and yet so light. Being on your own. He felt the need to pause for a moment, and sat on the low wall that bordered the garden of Rowan Cottage. Scots pine trees cast slabs of shadow across the garden. The water in the birdbath shimmered. Spikes of buddleia swelled in the moonlight. The skin of the mannequin looked slippery. A shiver rattled through his body despite the humidity of the night.

He noticed a long shape on the grass and then a line of smoke which trickled upwards from it. The shape moved slightly and he realized he was looking at Carl Ferry's hand as it reached for the cigarette in his mouth. He was lying flat on his back, statue-still, eyes open to the sky. Alan's stomach shifted with the shock and embarrassment of being caught staring into the garden. But the guy was unaware of him; on another planet. On an artist's planet. Alan tiptoed back to the road and walked on. A hundred yards further on, a spurt of laughter erupted from the bottom of his stomach. By the time he got home he was doubled over and in pain. He had to loosen the waist of his nurse's uniform in order to get his breath back. The boys would love this one.

• • • • • • • • • • • • • • • • • •

In early September, Alan went to Glasgow for an interview at the college he'd applied to. His friend Doonsie from a couple of villages away went with him, lured by the promise of a night out in the big city. To kill time before the bus home, they ventured into the Gallery of Modern Art which one of the lecturers had recommended to Alan. It would just be a quick glance.

They scuffled down the aisles between the exhibits. Alan noticed some art college types; dyed hair and small black notebooks, peering at things – taking their time over it. There were photos of thin people in Africa who seemed to be waiting for something; a horse made out of old bicycle parts, and then a painting that caught his eye. It was large and dark. A moon hung full in the branches of a tree and bounced its light off the shapes of two strange figures. Something soft-soled climbed Alan's spine as he leant into it for a better look. Recognition sprang him upright again. He'd seen this before – been part of the odd quality of the scene, understood its mystery. He felt the shiver for a second time.

'What's up?' asked Doonsie.

'This is Carl Ferry's.' He bent for confirmation from the label.

'You know him?'

In the village they thought they did; as much as they wanted to anyway. A guy with an untidy garden who lay on his back under the moon and didn't seem to need company. They'd painted a character for him, but Alan had never actually spoken to the guy. Did they know him?

'No – not really.'

As the bus crawled along the bay on the way home, Alan was jolted out of his doze. He saw the reason – tourist cars stopped at jaunty angles, blocking the road. He saw the travellers' encampment on the beach – kids, trailers, bicycles – funny how their arrival hardly raised a comment. But then they'd been coming to the same place for centuries for the winkle-picking. He saw how the evening sun illuminated the purple heather slope. It tumbled into the orange field of seaweed revealed by the low tide. He'd never noticed these two colours side by side before. Divided only by the narrow strip of road, they vibrated off each other. Who would have thought of putting them together? It wasn't really surprising that tourists felt the need to capture it on film. He would have liked to get off the bus to gaze at it for half an hour. But he had Doonsie with him.

'So. What did you think?' asked his mum. 'Will they give you a place?'

'I don't know yet.'

•   •   •   •   •   •   •   •   •   •   •   •   •   •   •   •   •   •

A few evenings after the gallery visit, Alan found a notebook lying in the lane near Rowan Cottage. He knew immediately who it belonged to. The pages were covered with lines and shade and blocks of colour and unreadable scribbles.

He couldn't post it through the letterbox because the door was already partially open. When he went to knock, it just gave a weak thud as it opened more. There was loud music coming from inside. Some classical stuff. It made him think of a giant figure taking massive angry strides within the walls of the cottage.

He put his head inside the door, shouted 'hello'. The front door opened directly into the kitchen but his view was blocked by a large canvas on an easel. A small table was multicoloured with tubes of paint and paint-blobbed cloths. Every surface contained one or two used cups or plates. A newspaper lay unopened on the floor. Perhaps he could get away with just tossing the notebook on the table and leaving – not intruding more into the artist's life. Carl Ferry stepped out from behind the board. He gave a little jump of surprise and Alan saw his lips move in 'hello' but heard nothing above the music.

'Prokofiev's *Romeo and Juliet* – The Montagues and Capulets,' said Carl Ferry after he had turned the volume down.

'Oh.' How was Alan supposed to respond to that? He held out the notebook. 'I found this on the road. Thought it might be yours.'

Carl Ferry put the paintbrush between his teeth and flicked though the pages. 'This old thing. Good of you. Thanks.' He put his brush down. 'I'm just taking a break. Stop for a cup of tea?'

Alan had wanted to retreat but some of the strangeness lifted, with Carl Ferry's welcome and the quietening of the room. 'Aye, great.' He stood just inside the door, hands thrust into jeans pockets. He noticed a press cutting taped onto the wallpaper opposite. 'Acclaim for Ferry's new *Moon People*'. The guy might be a nutter but he was a famous one.

'Carl Ferry,' he stepped towards Alan with an outstretched hand.

'I'm Alan – Alan Nicholson.'

'Live near?'

'Just up the road – Torrance Farm.'

'Oh, aye.' He started to roll a cigarette, then pressed his clothes with both hands, looking for matches. 'Have a seat.'

'Thanks.' Alan took in more of the room – the sketch pads and notes and canvas frames scattered across the table. There was more industry in this house than you realized from the outside. 'How're you enjoying Rowan Cottage?'

'Great. Quiet and space. Essential ingredients in my line.'

'It's a great wee place; nice garden.'

'I don't have much time for gardening. As you can probably tell.' They laughed.

'So what was it brought you here?'

'It's everyone's dream, isn't it? West coast. Living near the sea. Freedom.'

Alan shrugged. Carl went to the kettle with two mugs but was distracted from making the tea by his canvas.

He gazed at it, hand on chin.

'Yep. I can work here – no distractions, no one to tell me how I should live.'

Alan leaned forward slightly so he could see the painting.

'It's the human spirit,' said Carl. Alan nodded but wondered what he meant. A figure was outlined in thick brush strokes in the centre, arms aloft, head down, legs pounding. It made him think of the music earlier. 'Everybody needs to dance,' Carl said.

Alan looked at the painting again. He really wanted the pounding figure to make some sense for him. Dance. Yes, there was something he could relate to. He recalled the way the pipes filled him when Ronnie played them late at night in the pub. The way he and the other boys would start stamping, the rhythm and the beer commanding their bodies even though they never thought of themselves as dancers. So you could put a feeling like that into a painting. Get it out of your body and onto a canvas. Like the shiver. You could paint a shiver.

'Aye.' He smiled.

Alan heard Robert's tractor chortle by as he was sitting with a cup of tea at Carl's kitchen table. What would the boys make of this? He felt the watchful gaze of a ring of familiar faces, thought of the circle of linked arms he'd been part of for *Auld Lang Syne* at the end of countless village hall dances. As a child he'd looked up at younger versions of men like Robert Mackinnon, gradually reached eye level with them. The grip within the circle tightened. The arms crossed in front of his chest constricted his breathing. He coughed.

'Sorry,' said Carl and wafted the smoke away from Alan.

'No, no, it's fine, it's not you.'

'Why didn't you offer to do his garden?' his Mum asked later. 'Needs taking in hand. The lawn's knee-high now. Would be a bit of extra money for you.'

'I may not be here much longer.'

'Oh, have you heard?'

'Not yet.'

•   •   •   •   •   •   •   •   •   •   •   •   •   •   •   •   •   •

It was Friday and Alan stood holding his pint in a circle of some of the boys of his own age. They shouted above the music, planted their big boots wide apart. They talked about the new girl Craig had started to see, how Rangers were doing, the lad in the next village in a head-on with a French tourist on the wrong side of the road. Robert and Willy Mackinnon were nearby, jabbing fat fingers and 'one things' at each other. Alan watched Malky, leaning on the bar, back to the crowd. His upper body was still and upright but the legs were wild in a jig behind him, following the urgency of the music. Then Malky grabbed a rail above him and pulled himself off the floor, starting to climb spider man feet up the front of the bar. When the barmaid prodded him in the stomach, he dropped back down and lunged over the bar to kiss her. The usual Friday night. The familiar circle.

There was an impulse in Alan. To shiver his arms free from the *Auld Lang Syne* embrace, maybe even to spit and stamp. He visualized the circle re-knotting to close the gap he left, saw himself stride away.

'And what is it you're going to be studying again?' Willy asked as he congratulated him with a dram brought over from the bar.

Alan only missed one beat before he replied. 'Art,' he said. 'With technical drawing as an option.'

Willy spluttered slightly into his beer and then looked at Alan. 'I'll tell you one thing. That's not going to get you a job on the fish farm.'

Keeping away from the water

She settled the kiss precisely onto the nicely defined line of his wrist muscle. The fair hairs on his forearms rasped against her face. He was sexy when he was driving – shades on, arms outstretched at the wheel. It felt grown up, being on holiday in a hire car with Dan. She had brought him here on his first trip to Scotland with his fishing rods in the back, like a little boy going on a seaside holiday.

'Christ, look at that, Morag,' he ducked back and forth, sharing his eyes between the road and the snow tops of the mountains way above them.

She picked up the toy zebra that was seated on its backside with rear legs splayed. It faced them on pub tables, on pillows in their hotels, and here on the dashboard of the car. She held it against Dan's cheek, jumping it towards him with small shuffles. Then he was feeling for his cigarettes, searching for the Madonna CD. He never just concentrated on driving, could never devote two hands to it. Dad used to be just the same at the wheel. Maybe men were like that. She offered a cube of chocolate towards his mouth. After looking at the block on her lap for a moment she put it back in the glove compartment without taking any herself. The sight of it made her feel queasy.

How much wine had she drunk last night? Surely not enough to feel like this. Perhaps it was one of those viruses, or hunger making her feel sick – too long since the full Scottish breakfast. She could hardly take in the flow of the landscape they were passing through – the land of her childhood. Her memories were numbed with nausea. Her head bobbed and nodded, led by heavy eyelids. She was fighting to stay awake, to take in what they'd come to see. Her senses thudded against the headrest, fences, sheep, rocky crags.

• • • • • • • • • • • • • • • • • •

Screaming, scattering chickens, I'm running in wellies that are too big. Don't look back, it loses time. I know he's close, can tell by the snorting behind me, and the voice, 'I'm coming for you, I'm coming Morag'. Round and round the white walls of the cottage. Keep them to the left. Through the vegetable beds, dug over for Spring, slimy with seaweed. A haze of horizontals. With each circuit there's Mum in freeze-frame at the door, I can hear her laughing. Then I'm caught by the waist, and sky and hill wheel around as I'm upside down, my face scratching at the shoulder of his coarse jumper, bouncing as he runs down the field towards the loch. The horse monster carrying me to his underwater den. Screaming. I laugh so hard that I wet myself.

Back in the house, school things have been whisked away and hidden under furniture, behind cupboard doors. And there's still two weeks of holiday stretching ahead of me.

•   •   •   •   •   •   •   •   •   •   •   •   •   •   •   •   •

She felt uncomfortable – her breasts were heavy; her legs stuck to the plastic seat through her black tights; her skirt crunkled up around her thighs. She opened the car window a little, saw a crack of true white cloud against the smoked glass version. Something crept in, some kind of smell that she couldn't identify; familiar and strange at the same time. She shut the window again despite being hot. She was reminded of the heat they generated together in bed, enough to steam up the windows of the tiny hotel room last night. 'It's you,' she'd said. 'You're like a wild beast.' And they laughed but it made her think how she no longer feared the bucking monster he became during sex. She'd got used to the sharp edges of a man – edges that could graze you – jaws, shoulder blades, hip bones, stubble.

Seeing him outside London was a novelty, it gave her a fresh perspective. Her time with him was rolled out into a run of days and nights rather than the intense snatches at home. Snatches were fun in one way – she still got a little rush of well-being when she met him in the hotel bar after he finished his shift in the kitchen. Sometimes he'd bring her a dessert, and he always had stories for her – the unexpected table for ten at two minutes to nine; running out of bread rolls and having to run to the supermarket; the large tip from the business man who'd clinched a deal over Dan's *salmon en croute*. She enjoyed his stories, the way he sparkled with them. She listened as she licked the cream from her spoon, as his workmates passed them with a wink. She felt comfortable with him these days. Thankfully, it felt the same away from home too. It had all become a little less mysterious now. She had the explorer's sense of ownership. She had discovered Dan.

Dan took the bend wide, half watching a large bird hovering above them. Her stomach lurched with the gravity.

'Stop,' she said. 'Stop, Dan.'

Dan skidded the car to a halt. 'What is it?' He was staring at the road straight in front of them.

She held her throat. 'It's OK. Carry on, carry on. I thought I was going to be sick.'

'You not feeling good?'

'I think I must have eaten something. I'm OK.' As they moved off again, her eyes closed against the flash of sunshine through tree trunks, pulsing into her hot head. She was melting. Sun through glass. Keeping the chill winds away, pretending it was summer out there when she knew it wasn't.

• • • • • • • • • • • • • • • • • •

The sudden heat at Easter fells sheep into panting heaps in the shade and drops gifts of frog spawn overnight into the pond. The grip of winter lifts with the early morning mist. I lie on my stomach and gloop the frog spawn with a stick, watching it froth and pulsate. The winds turn sweet and soft, luring everyone out of winter dank cottages to breathe again, the air still clear of summer's midges. Doors and windows are opened wide for the spring to sweep through, rocking chairs and lifting papers from table to table, leaving the house smelling of wild garlic and the sea. Down the hill, boats are being re-floated in the loch, our neighbours stand and stare at the soil, appealing to their cold gardens to revive. Birds are careless; tumbling and falling down the steep gap to the water.

Voices burble up with the spring wind, with the sunshine, in the birch trees. I hear them best if I lay my head in the whipping grasses and close my eyes. They never quite let me hear them directly – who they are, what they're saying. I crunch down on last year's bracken by the burn, finding primroses among the rusty deadness, turning their pale faces to be licked by the sun. I try to see what's behind the veil of water, where the singing's coming from. I peer into dark corners of saturated black and jewel green moss, waiting for the chatter to transform into words.

At night I sit on Dad's lap before bed, listening to his story, telling him about the puzzles and discoveries of my day. 'They're just teasing you,' he says.

• • • • • • • • • • • • • • • • • • • •

'Fuck's sake.' The car juddered and swerved her out of her drowse. A sheep was walking in front of them, down the middle of the road, ears pressed back, casting its head, rolling its eyes back from left to right. It was nervous, looking for escape.

'No road sense these locals,' he said. 'Hey, you can't go to sleep. I thought you wanted to play the tour guide?'

'I do, I do.' She wriggled upright. 'Look, there's a sign for heather honey, just like I'd said there'd be.'

'U-huh. Geoff brought in a book of recipes that

use honey last week. Did I tell you?'

'No.'

'Amazingly versatile you know.'

'Yeah?'

'For glazing vegetables; put it with whisky in ice-cream; with vinegar in tomato sauces. Loads of things you can do with it. I guess heather honey would taste a bit different, do you think?'

As they talked, she stretched out a hand and stroked the back of his head. He leant into it, smiling, cat-like. He was such a foodie. When he had Sunday mornings off, they lazed in bed with a cafetière of coffee and blueberry muffins that he got up to make himself, so they were still warm. The bed, with him in it, the zebra, the muffin crumbs under them, felt like the safest place in the world. It was in this newly found den, when she talked about her childhood, that they'd hatched the plan for a holiday in the highlands.

Her fingers raked his floppy hair. She felt something gritty close to his scalp. It wasn't dandruff, it was much harder than that, like sand, as if he'd been swirled through sand-flecked waves.

Rain slammed against the windscreen, draining all the colour outside. Winter returned as they had their first glimpse of the loch. The loch that was too deep to find the bottom of. She shivered slightly, and closed her eyes again.

• • • • • • • • • • • • • • • •

On the beach with Anne. Anne who stays over sometimes during the holidays. We look for the smooth flat pebbles, the ones that spin best. We compete for the most bounces. Mine always go furthest because Dad has taught me how to flick my wrist, how to send the stones hopping out into the middle of the loch. You just see the tiny white flecks of spray against the dark hills opposite as the strides diminish and weaken. I get seven. Anne gets five. I count to eight the next time and it's still bouncing. We both watch, me jumping up and down, shrieking, 'It's a record, it's a record.' We both watch the white points scud into the far distance. But now they're not against dark hills. They're lost against a bigger area of angry foam out of which the head of something rises question-like, a long neck, a head erect turning towards us. Far, far out. We clutch each other's hands and run, run back up the hill to the cottage, lungs bursting, silent to each other until we find Mum and Dad. They seem to believe us.

Anne never comes to play again. Two days later Dad goes out on that fishing trip.

* * * * * * * * * * * * * * * * * *

'Hey, look at that. It must be loaded with fish. That's this afternoon sorted, then.'

She felt the grin turned towards her and opened her eyes to see the surface of the loch ruffled by west winds, gently rolling waves onto a pink shore. Still vast despite the years since she'd seen it, the loch was speckled and patchworked by the reflection of sunshine and showers above. A silver blue smooth strip of water shone against the dark of the far shore. It looked familiar. The road along the lochside was familiar too. It twisted and turned them, allowing them to snatch views of the loch between the birch outcrops on the banks.

She searched in her memory and on the roadside for the particular markers, the ones that used to tell her they were nearing home after a shopping trip to Inverness. They used to count them off, her and Dad. There was the leaping donkey sign swinging in the wind, where they'd turn to each other and say 'Eee-aw'; the roofless steading with the knobbly tree spiralling up inside it; the bungalow they saluted, whether or not the old man was there, the one who straightened from his digging to salute every passing car; and finally, just on the corner of their track where Dad slowed the car to climb to the cottage over the rocks and ruts, was the Witch Tree. It had a long head of hair that was blown almost horizontal and frozen into stone. The branches were grey and looked brittle, snappable. Whatever the wind was doing, the witch's hair was always blown in one direction.

But the markers didn't appear. Not yet anyway.

• • • • • • • • • • • • • • • • • •

The digger fills in the pond, dropping cakes of peat heavy onto the frogspawn. But I don't care, if it takes the water away. I play behind the cottage now, only in the places where you can't see the loch; the water that took Daddy away. Or I play in the house, back turned to the windows, with books and drawings and jigsaw puzzles that Mum buys for me in Inverness. I dream at night, dream that someone has scratched on a sandy beach a huge horse with a tiny rider on its back. And I'm near the edge of the water when a wave gallops towards me and I turn and run, seeing over my shoulder that it rears over me, keeps pace with me, threatening to suck me back in. It follows me towards the cottage until I wake.

I become a thief, leave school every day, pockets heavy with plasticine torn off from the flat wide strips in new packets in the classroom store. After Mum thinks I'm in bed, I roll the plasticine into warm balls, squeeze them into every crack in the wood, every eye in the floorboards, every gap between skirting board and wall, anywhere they'll fit. I close up the house, little by little, in the night. I begin to make it secure. I listen out for hooves pounding on turf – a sound which will launch me back under the bedclothes.

Early morning gulls mewl down the chimney. Their messages ricochet off its walls before dropping onto the cold hearth. A hole too big for plasticine. My eyes open onto a throng outside my window, golden green, floating in the sunlight, wings just starting to part in the sun. Mum finds me sheltering amongst dusty suitcases and the pots Granny gave her in the cupboard under the stairs.

'I need curtains. They're at the window, trying to get in, trying to get me to go out.'

When she takes me to the window in my bedroom she says, 'It's buds on the apple tree, darling. Being tossed on the wind. That's all.' She strokes my hair, says we'll get curtains anyway, nice heavy ones so I won't wake too early. But I notice for the first time that she smells salty, like seawater, which make me wonder if I should believe her. She never does get the curtains anyway, because soon afterwards we pack up the house and move away. A long way away.

•   •   •   •   •   •   •   •   •   •   •   •   •   •   •   •   •

Dan accelerated on a new stretch of straight road, channelled through the rock, where the trees had been obliterated from the sides of the loch. As she looked over the water, something stirred. Something stirs from very deep. At first the only mark it makes on the surface is a darkening – a darkening under a stretch of clear blue sky. Morag frowns and watches the mark on the water. It grows restless, almost hairy looking, rough, as though the water's starting to boil. She leans forward, sweeps beads of sweat away from her forehead, puts a hand across her mouth. The darkness begins to swell. It breaks the surface of the water, turning a dark smooth shiny wheel slow through the water.

'Stop, stop,' she shouted.

Dan pulled across and slammed the brakes on. 'Don't be sick in the car, honey.'

But she was already out, pushing through some spriggy birches which blocked the clear view of the loch. She scrambled down the bank, her heels catching and sliding on the rough wet ground, her clothes snatched by the branches.

'Where are you going?' Dan called, half out of the car.

As she regains a clear view of the loch, the vast eel-like back rises and sinks again below the surface, suggesting a neck and head, before she reels forward and vomits hard, falling onto her knees in the wet grass.

Dan knelt next to her, his hand on her back, stroking her as she shivered. She wiped her hands on the wet grass and ran them across her face, then rocked onto her heels and looked back across the now still loch.

The air is salty. A burn clatters into the loch down rocky steps nearby, a chatter of voices behind it. Chattering without words. And then she hears the matching whisper from her own belly. A whisper soft and discreet; one she should have let herself hear before. She reaches deep, into a very different territory, and finds several new certainties.

She looked into Dan's face, reached out to grip her hands on either side of it. 'Dan, don't go fishing. Please don't go fishing.'

'It's all right,' he laughed. 'Don't worry. Plenty more days yet. I won't leave you on your own this afternoon.'

'No, no, it's not that.'

'Maybe you should go and lie down somewhere?'

But she couldn't capture words to explain. It was serious for her and for Dan. It was grown up. He mustn't be taken from them. 'Dan, I think we should go away from here. Right away. Away from the water.'

Dan straightened from his squat and held a hand out to help her up. 'Sure,' he said.

She clung to him as they scrambled back up the slippery bank and she didn't look at the loch again.

Death Wish

Will it be your body or the rucksack they find first? The rucksack, unfastened and abandoned. Left on a rocky outcrop not far off the path, next to a half-drunk bottle of Vittel water and a small pile of orange peel. Without that clue it could take ages before you're discovered in the thick forest below. It must be a fall of five hundred metres. Straight down the sun-kissed cliff. Perhaps it'll be a walker who comes across you. With tanned legs and dusty boots, he'll be reclaiming the path from melt-water landslides in the spring sunshine. He'll recoil from the lacerated limbs, still hanging heavy in the low branches. The discovery might take long enough that it's the smell that makes him notice. He'll run for help, making uneven progress as the retches fold him double.

There's a third possibility, beyond the discovery of the body or the rucksack. The hotel staff will notice the bed unslept in. The first night they'll shrug away a holiday romance, but after the second, they'll call in the police. They need to be paid if the room's not occupied.

But it's most likely to be the rucksack that leads to the body. A group of scouts from Switzerland sent off for the day to practise their map-reading skills will see it when they pass in the morning. They won't think much of a small rucksack left near the path. But when they retrace their steps later, and it's still there, they'll cluster around its open top, not touching, but peering in as if the contents will reveal what they should do. They'll debate it for a while, until one of them is bold enough to pick it up, clip up the straps, and carry it down to the town. It will end up with the police and trigger a search party to swarm through the forest below.

For the detective it'll be a 'Lucky Bag' of sorts. He'll fix his eyes on the wall in front, as his fingers close blind on each item, unpacking them onto the Formica table. When he's sure it's empty, he'll put the rucksack on one side and frown at the collection on the table.

Sun cream; factor eight. (When they find the body, perhaps they'll notice the two red patches on the upper arms where the rucksack worked with sweat to rub off the cream and allow the sun to bite.)

A French-English dictionary. The Larousse mini series; practical and lightweight.

A jumper. Orange and woollen. Hand-framed in Scotland.

Sunglasses. (But you'll still be wearing them perhaps? Posing in Raybans even to the death.)

A small sponge bag. Lipstick and tampons inside. Female, then (my dear Watson).

A map of Lac d'Annecy.

A wallet. (The detective will feel more confident of an ID now.) French Francs inside, but no cards, no papers. Left behind in the security of a hotel room.

Two postcards. Unwritten. One is an aerial shot of the lake enclosed by its amphitheatre of peaks. Colour a bit brash. The other shows the pretty canal-side and its terrace bars in the old town of Annecy. (The Coroner, brought over from Britain to conduct the investigation, will resist a moment's guilt as he or she takes a beer there in the evening, enjoying the sunshine and the drift past of smiling tourists. You have to take a break from death.)

A plastic carrier bag with the remains of a baguette, a piece of cheese, (Emmenthal), and a Swiss Army Knife.

A black and red hard-backed notebook. Ruled.

The notebook. Without it they'll know nothing. All they'll know is that you're British (or at least English-speaking), female, apparently on holiday. And then the notebook will take away all the mystery. They'll get to know you with unearned ease. It might not provide your name, address, next of kin, but it will identify you. They'll know where you've been. They might even mark your route with those fat pins with coloured heads on a map on the inquiry room wall. And they'll stand and gaze at the pattern. 'No ordinary holiday, that. As if she was running from something,' they'll say.

They'll know what you've been doing – the days sitting alone at café tables, dragging your rucksack in and out of trains and buses. Hanging your washed-through underwear overnight on a piece of string tied between radiator and wash-stand in the hotel room. They'll know how you felt when you looked at your cold sores in the mirror, and pulled the two grey hairs from your fringe. They'll know about your tussle with sleep and the encounters with long-forgotten people in your dreams.

And they'll know what it is you've done; what it was that dispatched you for a 'short break' to France. They'll know how you killed in cold blood. The way you just wanted it dead. And the people who shadow you since, waiting to punish, pushing you to the edge. And how you knew they were there, even though they hid, appearing only as a penumbra, a shady outline, behind bus drivers, waiters, fellow tourists.

When they find the body, they'll identify you with the help of your chipped front tooth. Your mother will choke into her hanky on the phone to the British Embassy. She'll remember not only the *fact* of the tooth, but *how* you chipped it. Running up the garden path in answer to her call, to see the kittens being born. You tripped and crashed onto the front step. But she cradled you in anyway, dripping tears and blood, to witness the mysterious moment. The high mews of new life in a cardboard box stilled your sobs. And afterwards she took you to an emergency dentist.

•   •   •   •   •   •   •   •   •   •   •   •   •   •   •   •   •   •

The air is sun-dried; the cool spring wind suspended by the rocks. Two butterflies chase each other, prettifying the vertical panorama. Sky, to Haute-Savoie peaks, to lake. You're small and still amongst the birds who tumble and glide in the thermals thrown up by the edge in front of you, the gap from cliff top to lake floor. They have the nonchalance of Dead Sea swimmers. Cars buzz along the hazy lakeside below, inhabiting a world of different perspectives; roadside restaurants, boat hire, and views only upwards.

You came from that world this morning, before you reached stillness here. Ducks cowered from the heat, their heads and necks swallowed by the lake. The grass in the low-lying meadows was starred with spring flowers like the Swiss chocolate boxes brought as presents from European airports in your childhood. The meadow beckoned you to tumble and roll in its length and moisture, to press your nose to the wild garlic. It tried to trick you, like the men in the town, with the fresh smell they left in the air as they passed you, their tanned faces crying out to be kissed. A pretence that it was safe to linger. But you resisted. Your feet continued upwards on the rocky path, the sweat drying on your face. Until you found this place among rocks and dry grass on the summit of the cliff. This is the place.

You peel an orange as you wait. The citrus oil bursts into your face, but these days, since the death, it no longer makes you feel sick. Your body is your own again. You can hear the dryness around you. The air crackles with it. The crispness of brush and branch betrays movement. You know that before long it'll be human movement. A noise halts your breathing; the lack of human voice as tangible as a shouted warning. But when you look over your shoulder, there's no one. A bird or lizard making small tracks through the grass. You breathe again, but the waiting hurts.

You wonder what will happen before the spread-eagle in blue air. It'll be a challenge for the coroner. Injuries consistent with a fall of so many metres. But did you step? Or slip? Or were you pushed?

The sun drowses your eyelids and your body succumbs to something like sleep. Your senses startle you awake when an ant's jaw closes on your bare calf or the dry panic of the undergrowth sits you upright, swivels your head. And the images are there again, breezing over you with the rise and fall of consciousness. You see your mother's back in the familiar herringbone overcoat. As she turns, she shows you a slight frown in a blank face, and then she walks on, away from you up the home street, her carrier bag concealing comforts from the corner shop.

Through the eyelashes, a flutter of blue sky, a crackle near your ear, and then you're looking up from a white bed, at a nurse, and she smiles and sinks a needle into your arm, casting you several leagues deep into feather pillows. And you wake up in another room, surrounded by women's bodies inert on trolleys, and a thick pad between your legs, stuck to you with what must be blood. And something is nudging to the front of your mind. A circumstance. A curled up body, shrimp-like, in a metal pan somewhere. You don't see it but you know you're responsible for it. You wanted to kill it. Wished it dead.

Then your eyes are blue-wide and they fix on the arc of a paraglider canopy, luminous green above you. It pirouettes, the human centre dark against the sun-green. Very dark. The pilot swings outwards to side-fill the canopy. He mocks you with his slowness, knowing that he must finally come down. He sweeps and circles, plays with the thermals, accelerating the threat high above you. His crossed legs beneath the harness become indiscernible. You know that he smiles, his head bent forward to observe his prey. And you're lizard-long in the sun near the cliff edge, face upwards. You lie and wait as he spirals up and up.

And there's a sense of relief; an end in sight. Ever

since the clinic, you've been in a series of endless waiting rooms, one adjoining the next. Waiting for the moment.

•   •   •   •   •   •   •   •   •   •   •   •   •   •   •   •   •   •   •

And when some hours have passed, the low sun has changed the colours on the lake and ruffled the oak woodland, mellowed the cliff colour. You see yourself as the shadowy paraglider must, standing on the extreme edge, facing outwards. And you're holding something high in both hands. Small petals break away from it, float outwards from your hands, bright against the shadows; dark against the lake glare. They dance in the light and the upward currents before taking a chaotic journey outwards and downwards towards the lake. As you tear and release the last pieces of notebook, you stand erect on the cliff top, arms stretched upwards, your stillness caught in the turn and curl of a galaxy of paper stars. You're ready now. And a small distance behind you, a rucksack lies open, waiting to be discovered.

Night Life

The white picket fence and dim street lamps guided Lorna to the gate at the edge of the town. She passed through it, out of her day-life and onto the station platform. The rails glinted, running out of the built-up area, towards the night eyes of the countryside. She breathed deeply, enjoying the prickle of frost on her skin, the dark embrace of the sky with its pinpoints of stars. Before bed she would pamper herself with a hot chocolate, or maybe even a beer, in the restaurant car. She'd let her thoughts ramble at will. There was nothing she had to concentrate on until eight am at Euston Station. Only after that would she have to squeeze herself in and out of dresses and shoes and decisions with Karen.

She didn't come to the station often. The town looked different from this side of the fence. It looked smaller – the buildings squashed in tight to each other by the hills rising on all sides. Smoke from the chimneys cocooned the town from the wide sky.

She passed under the wrought iron bridge to find someone was already there. So, she wouldn't have the platform, even the train, to herself after all. It was bound to be someone she knew, someone who would keep her leashed to the world the other side of the gate. They'd gossip about Geoff Davidson, caught flashing outside the Brownies' hut; the local meat war escalating over cut-price venison sausages; the latest teenage pregnancy. They'd dig deeper and deeper into people's lives with the liberty of travelling far from them. It had happened to her before. It was as if she carried a hometown brand mark on her forehead. An inescapable marking.

The man leant away from her towards a notice board on the wall. He wore a tweed overcoat, a scarf wrapped high up his neck, and a hat, one of those flat-topped, broad-rimmed Latin American ones. His face was shaded by it. An expensive looking soft leather suitcase lay on the bench. This was no local.

'Hi there.'

'Ah hello.' He turned a little stiffly and smiled. 'I'm not the only one getting on here then. I was beginning to doubt there was a train. Deserted, this place.' He traced a circle in the air with a gloved hand. He had a slightly crumpled face, lined, but pleasant. It seemed rude to walk further down the platform now, even though she knew she would have to when the train pulled in. She struggled her rucksack off and put it on the ground.

'Let's hope it's on time. It's usually not bad.'

'You're a regular?'

'Been on it a few times.'

'So ... you live at this end or that?'

She was conscious of his eyes piercing the gloom. 'This end. How about you?'

'On my way back to London. Well, somewhere ...' He seemed distracted by a search in his overcoat pocket. He pulled out a packet of cigarettes and paused while he lit one. The way he drew on it struck her as aristocratic. He nodded his head over the railway line in the direction of the river. 'Been working at the theatre for a couple of weeks.'

'Oh. What was on? I know – *The Woman in Black?*'

'Yes,' he smirked. 'You saw it?'

'No. Terrible isn't it. You never go when it's on your doorstep. Just heard. In fact heard it was very good. You an actor?'

'Yes.' The drawl again, a puff on the cigarette from a long erect neck. 'For my sins. And you? You live around here – what is there for a young woman in these parts?' He seemed to study her face closely, leaning more into the centre of the lamplight which encircled them and their luggage.

'Nothing glamorous like acting. I teach. At the local secondary – I'm an art teacher.' He carried on looking, as if it required more explanation, and then swiped his head upwards. The profile of a muzzle stretched into the night sky, formed by the brim of his hat, his nose, the mist of his breath.

'I loved it here. So different, so beautiful.' He gestured at the dark summits reaching towards the stars, not letting you forget where you were. 'But you *live* here. Fascinating.' He returned his gaze to her.

'Someone has to.'

The rails vibrated beside them, the screeched signal approached. 'Here it comes.' She heaved her rucksack onto one shoulder.

He turned to gather up his bag but she could feel his head was towards her, feel a question still hanging in the air.

'Come and have a glass of wine with me in the bar. I'd love to know more about teaching. In a place like this.'

'OK.' She didn't hesitate, she was going anyway. And she'd never had a drink with an actor before.

'I'm Jeremy.'

'Lorna.'

They shook hands and turned towards the train. It lumbered lengthy into the station, elegant from Inverness, bringing the promise of uniformed guards, sponge bags on the beds, and the swaying restaurant car. It wasn't utilitarian, like modern travel. You climbed aboard an Edwardian fantasy. As the train passed, Lorna felt as if a gush of steam wrapped them, obscuring the everyday setting of the station. The guard leant out of the window.

'Carriage K,' he called.

'That's me.' She started to pursue the carriage down the platform.

'I'm C. I'll see you in the bar.'

• • • • • • • • • • • • • • • • • •

He was already seated with his cigarettes and silver lighter on the white tablecloth in front of him when she arrived.

He was leaning back, laughing with the waitress who was uncorking a bottle of wine. Two glasses were already set out. Not, she noticed, the usual plastic ones. He seemed to know the waitress' name. She had a toothy smile and giggled with her shoulders.

He stood up slightly when he saw Lorna coming and extended an open hand towards the seat opposite. She slipped into the seat, fixed to the floor. It gave her no choice but to sit square opposite him. The wine glasses, tablecloth, waiters, seemed suddenly to thrust them into intimacy, more a table for two than a drink at the bar. He poured wine into her glass, giving the bottle the small final twist that she'd seen people do.

'Cheers,' he clinked her glass. His eyes seemed to catch on one of her manicured hands before he refocused on her face. The hand was still marked faintly with purple ink where she'd written 'SEED' to remind her to buy bird seed on the way home from work. She hated to see the birds go hungry once the ground was hard with frost.

He sat back again, breathed out heavily and reached for his cigarettes. 'Do you mind? I've had a hell of a week.'

'No. Me too.'

The first taste of wine dropped her shoulders, sent a shudder of relaxation through her. It was good to be spoilt like this. To be travelling in style without everyday baggage. In fact almost forgetting you were travelling. A maroon-clad waiter passed their table.

'Two cheeseburgers, a pot of tea and a hot chocolate,' Lorna heard behind her.

'Right you are.'

'I've never been on one of these before. It's like the Orient Express, eh?' A woman's voice cackled.

'Hopefully no murders though, madam. Tends to cause a delay.'

Jeremy was looking at her over his cigarette. He seemed to creak with each movement. To creak with leather and expensive textiles. He must be twenty-five years older than her, maybe even thirty, she thought. He pulled his tie loose with one hand. He seemed a long way away and with the background engine noise, she wondered how easy conversation was going to be. She was good at small talk but this might be a challenge.

'So tell me about being a teacher. In the beautiful Highlands.' He leant forward and smiled and she responded to his questions about how she got kids to be creative, taking them to galleries in the cities, how she found working in the battle zone of teenage hormones. She told him how she had got used to being in the staff room with people who had been her own teachers at the same school. How being a teacher made you famous in a small place, you were recognized everywhere you went – a minor celebrity. You got invited onto committees and asked to judge Women's Rural Institute competitions. And people watched out for you too. In a small place, you were cared for.

In return she quizzed him about the life of an actor, all the travelling to strange theatres, the uncertainties of work for the next month. It was interesting. She forgot about the hard week at work. She forgot about the matching magazines she and Karen had bought at opposite ends of the country and the long telephone conversations in which they'd referred each other to page numbers, colours, shoe styles, in preparation for this weekend. When the train clanked to a stop in another dimly lit station, she was surprised to see the sign for Perth. Perth was where she went for shopping and the cinema, just forty minutes down the A9 from home. It was incongruous, as if the rails of the night train had taken her right out of her normal life.

'You live in London?'

'Hah.' He took a puff of his cigarette and leaned forward as if a long story was coming. 'I did. Things may be a bit different when I get back though.'

'Meaning?' Maybe it was the wine that made her so forward, made her more curious than she would normally be with a stranger. He looked at her sidelong from baggy eyes and his voice seemed to have a slight alcoholic slur.

'Yes. There have been a few changes. I might go away for a bit. Perhaps Italy.'

'How lovely.' She pictured sunshine, piazzas, and men in boats singing about ice creams. 'Will you be acting there?'

'At the moment, my dear, I haven't a bloody clue what I'll be doing.' He was refilling their glasses and she found herself gulping at the wine, trying to keep up with him.

'So ... why leave London?'

'Wife trouble. Hitting the buffers I think you might call it.' He laughed.

'I'm sorry.'

He leant forward over the lighter which he played with in his hands. They were large and rough hands, more physical than she would have expected in an actor.

'No, no. Natural really. Kids all flown the nest. Both wanting our own lives again. I'm happy to go.'

'But you don't know where to?'

'See what happens when the guard pulls me out of bed tomorrow morning.'

She considered what that sort of freedom might feel like. Maybe you got more spontaneous with age, rather than less. Although this didn't seem to be borne out by the routines of her parents, who were more reliable than the train timetable.

He dropped his head towards his hands, rubbing his fingers through the thick wool of his hair, smoothing it back from his face. He wasn't going to cry was he? She was used to being a magnet to the no-hopers in her local pub – men who'd been thrown out, made redundant – poor souls who'd lost everything including their self respect. They cried on her shoulder, wallowed over her, their breath harsh with whisky or vomit. They'd bring their stools close to hers as they lost the plot with the boys at the bar, whisper their secrets, collapse their chins onto their chests in misery. Looking moon-like into her eyes they'd say, 'Thanks for understanding, hen'. And they never wanted to know anything about her. She was happy to be the mopper up. But she'd never expected to be consoling a man like this.

He sat back upright, springing out of his dark thoughts, and re-filled their glasses. 'Don't run away. Gotta go to the loo.' His speech was unmistakably slurred.

She was feeling slightly drunk herself now, heady with the wine and unfamiliar situation. She breathed deeply and smoothed her hair back over her shoulders, releasing it from its clasp. She realized on looking around that they were the only customers left. The staff were slouched around a table on the other side of the glass screen consuming hot chocolate and soup. They seemed to be off-duty, their Edwardian professionalism discarded over the backs of their chairs with their maroon jackets. The playing cards were out – it looked like the beginning of an all-night session. They laughed and glanced over their shoulders up the carriage. She felt they were complicit in her tête-à-tête. They must know she and Jeremy had got on separately, had formed this apparent intimacy in the last hour.

It was late, but she felt no inclination to go to her cabin, felt a different person from the one who'd left the school a few hours earlier. She imagined getting off the train in London the next morning, walking away from the dress fittings, taking a train to Heathrow and choosing a flight to somewhere, anywhere.

He ordered another bottle of wine when he came back. That seemed to commit her further to the situation. The Borders passed by invisibly, an occasional reminder from a row of orange lights. The windows on either side of them reflected back the picture of their heads, close among empty tables. As she looked into the reflection nearest to her, she noted the shine in her dark hair, the way the glass smoothed worry from her face. She seemed to look quite different from the Lorna that she saw in the mirror at home – sleeker, more glamorous. Then her eyes met his in the glass. Heat pricked her face and she turned back to him, as if the dark glass and softness of the reflection had allowed him to see more than she wanted.

'Nice hair … loose like that.' He lit another cigarette. 'Married, are you?'

She rejected the possibility that his eyes had slithered off her face and over her body. 'No, plenty of time for all that.'

'Boyfriend?'

'Not at the moment, no.'

'What is it takes you to London?'

'Shopping. For a friend's wedding actually. She's from here … there, I mean.' She gestured backwards along the tracks. 'I'm to be bridesmaid – have to choose dresses, shoes, all that stuff …'

'Very good.' He sat back and observed her. 'I didn't think young people bothered getting married these days. Conventional you country girls, hmm?'

'And hopefully while I'm there maybe get out to a film, go dancing.' This still sounded boring. She set out, mentally, on a rapid tour of seedy bars, clubs, somewhere she might be offered drugs, wear a short dress with bootlace straps, a studded collar even. Things she should do in London rather than the rounds of wedding boutiques. Inspiration came. 'Might get a tattoo done.'

'Ooh.' He wriggled slightly in his seat. 'Where?'

'Oh there's bound to be places in Camden …' She stopped when she caught his smirk. 'Oh, I see what you mean. Well, that would be telling, eh?' She teased him, he wouldn't make her seem strait-laced and boring so easily.

He sprung forward in his seat, eyes wide. 'I wonder what they'll have to say about that back home?'

'Well, they might not see it, might they?' She revelled in the thought of eyes on her at the swimming pool, eyes trying to get a glimpse of the dagger on her shoulder blade, the snake coiling around her navel, or maybe it should be 'love' and 'hate' on the curve of each buttock. They'd need the glimpse to establish whether the rumours were true. In the no-man's land of train travel, this almost seemed possible – returning to them all as a slightly different person. She almost laughed out loud thinking of the chorus line of gasps lisping through the town. The men in the pub would have something to say about it, once a few pints had loosened tongues. But some people might not meet her eye, might think it unsuitable for a teacher. 'And if they don't like it, they can go fuck themselves,' she thought. But it became an out-loud thought. Her voice sounded strange. Strangely angry. And a bit drunk.

'Oh, so the highland heritage home can get a bit wearing?'

Naming it had made her light-headed – it turned more of her out loud. 'Well, it's pretty hard to … you know … to do anything without being noticed.' To do anything naughty, she thought. 'When you've got uncles and aunties and the whole of form 2B watching you eat your muesli.' She tried to laugh, but felt like a schoolgirl, embarrassed. 'I'm just joking,' she said slurping at her wine. 'Too much of this.'

But he ignored her dismissal. 'So. What are you going to do about it? Why don't you leave?'

This jarred. Jarred as if Karen, her parents, colleagues were hearing it. 'Like I say, it was a joke. I don't want to leave. I love the place, it's my home. I've a good job … you know, you can't have everything.'

He stretched a hand towards her face and traced a finger from her hairline, down the forehead to the top of her nose. She knew there was the beginning of a wrinkle there. His finger felt slightly sharp, like a claw dragging at her skin.

'No good denying yourself,' he whispered. 'Twist

you up. Tear you about inside. Show up in places like this.'

His baggy face was too close to hers now and his breath a bit ragged. She could smell him, a feral kind of smell. Her eyes flicked away from him down the carriage. Seeing the group of off-duty guards made her aware of how this must look to them. How had she got herself into this situation – being mauled by a man she'd only met an hour or so ago? Being pushed to exposures by too much wine. She sat back to escape his hand. If she could have moved the seat she would have done, moved it so she wasn't square to him – eye to eye, face to face, chest to chest. He sat back in his chair too but stretched his long legs under the table. She had to move her feet to one side to avoid tangling with his.

Lorna remembered reading somewhere about men who got turned on by train journeys. Delusions of *Brief Encounter* glamour – women needing help or love. And worse still, she remembered the picture in her father's *Penthouse* magazine of a middle-aged man accosted by a group of school girls on a train, having sex in the toilets. This man, professional, tweedy, her father's age, he couldn't be suffering from such delusions could he? She'd never have allowed herself to get drunk with him if she'd suspected such a motive.

'Come to a gallery with me tomorrow.'

To stand up and walk away seemed rude. He was just being friendly wasn't he? Nothing untoward had happened. You couldn't jump to conclusions. And he'd paid for all the wine. 'I thought you were going to Italy.'

'Come to Italy then.'

She tittered.

He mumbled something which she thought sounded like 'Come and be naughty.' His hands padded one at a time across the table towards her, his eyes fixing hers, unblinking. His smell got stronger, musky, like someone who lives with dogs. When his hands reached her side of the table, she stood up.

'I'm going to bed now. Thanks for the wine.'

He looked up at her from his slump across the table, then wobbled up himself. What could she say to bring the conversation back to one that was suitable for their circumstances, for strangers who have passed the time chatting on a train?

'It was nice to meet you.' She held out her hand. Manners like her mother had taught her.

He ignored her hand. 'I'll look you out. When I'm up-country again. Or why don't you come to the Palladium? *Love's Labour's Lost* next month.'

So all that stuff about going away – a fabrication then. She nodded vaguely. 'Bye then,' she tried to turn away before he pinned her to phone numbers or addresses. But he caught her shoulders between his hands, kissed her first on one cheek and then on the other. He lingered over each one. She felt his cheek saggy and soft against hers, like she remembered her grandmother's being. Sticky, almost.

'Goodnight,' she said to the table of staff as she passed, conscious that she was finding it difficult to walk straight. They looked up at her and she felt their judging eyes, and noticed that they refocused just behind her.

'Goodnight sir,' one of them said, and she realized Jeremy was in her trail, prowling along behind her, head down and swaying.

The guard exchanged glances with Lorna. 'I think you'll find your cabin's the other way, sir. Carriage C, sir.'

Jeremy fumbled for the ticket inside his jacket. She took the opportunity to escape, bumping her shoulders against each wall as she almost ran down the narrow corridor. She checked behind her until she reached the safety of her cabin and locked the door.

• • • • • • • • • • • • • • • • • •

'We're going to Liberty first, then John Lewis at two. We can have lunch there.'

Karen and Lorna met as planned for a coffee

before starting the shopping trip. Lorna was exhausted by Karen's energy after only twenty minutes. She wanted all the news, the gossip about home. Their conversation express-trained Lorna back the five hundred miles she had come.

'Didn't you sleep very well? You look spaced out, girl.'

Things did seem to be moving very slowly, the ground undulating a bit like it did after a few days at sea. She shaded her eyes from the sun that flashed through the café window off passing cars, too bright and glaring for her, as if she'd just surfaced from underground. The previous night now seemed remote, almost something she could laugh about. Just some weirdo on the train. But she didn't share it with Karen. Not yet. Not until she'd dealt with the new awareness prodding away inside her. It was as if she had 'discovered' a Himalayan mountain, a new high peak. It had been there all along really, but when a courageous explorer records it, it can never be lost again. You have to put it on the map.

'No, I didn't sleep too well actually. Sorry.'

'Soon wake you up.'

'Yes, I think you might. Karen, do you fancy going out somewhere?'

'Tonight you mean. I thought you were tired?'

'I am. But it's Saturday isn't it? In the big city.'

'OK, why not. We'll have earned it by then.'

Lorna saw the day stretching ahead of her. A landscape covered with lace and silk and frills, that she had to find the least painful route through.

'And could I slip off to Camden Town for an hour or so? Can you spare me? There's something I need to do there.'

Underbelly

While we were watching the band, I only drank two bottles of beer. Or was it three? Anyway, enough to feel a bit jolly and have a bop about, but not enough to bring on a Kafka-esque transformation. Judy and I are on the pavement outside the City Hall afterwards, having our usual moan about the office.

'Hanging around the stage door like groupies, at our age,' she says as we watch the crowd fill up the pavement and disperse. An insect-like swarm of elbows rise as denim jackets are shivered on over T-shirts. That's early summer for you – the temperature doesn't anywhere like meet the long stretch of pale blue evening light.

'Where to next?' I ask.

'Sorry, Sheila, can't do. I told the babysitter I'd be back by eleven. Have to rush.'

'Don't worry. I could do with an early night.'

She gives me a quick hug and turns maternal resolution towards her car.

• • • • • • • • • • • • • • • • • •

An early night? Ten forty-five pm and cold on the pavement. Reminds me of going to my first gig, when I missed the main band completely because Dad said I was only allowed to go if he collected me at ten-thirty. Ten-thirty! The finger of embarrassment still tickles me after all those years.

I find my Mini, hiding behind the real cars, and start to head home. I like to sing while I drive but I can't remember the words of the songs we've just heard. So full blast Virgin Radio has to do. An old Van Morrison song, *Moondance*, comes on through the crackle.

'What a marvellous night for a moondance ...'

He's right. It would be. Traffic lights on red

punctuate my flow. A couple laugh into each other's faces as they drift across the road. She wears a white mini skirt, displays locust-thin legs. Here's me on my way home to bed when they're just off to a club or something. Another beer and I'd go too. Even on my own. Forget myself on the dance floor, let it all hang out. Well, most of it.

• • • • • • • • • • • • • • • • • • •

I leave the city limits and propel the Mini through the unlit narrow roads leading home. I know the route well. I like the way I can swing the car round, hands firm and close together on the small leather-covered wheel. The tyres stick to the road; no give or slide as we power round the corners. I use the gears, changing between third and fourth to keep the revs up. Expert. Tight and hard. Egged on by beer and my own internal movie soundtrack. I am as skilled as, what's his name – is it Aston Martin? No, that's a car. As skilled as Stirling Moss.

As I start on the series of tight bends through the village, *Losing my Religion,* by REM comes on the radio.

I like this one. The words swell up from the bottom of my stomach, burst out of my mouth, demand more speed. The radio's so loud I can only just hear my own voice. But I know I'm shouting by the way my face muscles feel stretched and by my light-headedness from gulping at air between the lines. And my foot is hard down, the engine racing, my small light car shining with confidence as we corner fast and hard.

As I streak towards the final right-hander, the song hooks a sharp tooth into my underbelly. It hurts. Exposes a chasm. Switches on the person who spends occasional dark hours doubled on the floor, battering fists and sobs into the carpet. My voice cracks; my foot reflexes harder onto the accelerator. I see the barbed wire fence and plumes of headlight-white grass coming for me. The chevron crisp and over-white. And why not? Why not keep going?

My foot relents onto the brake, my right shoulder presses hard against the window as my whole body urges the bend. Afterwards I slow down. My pulse races. The high is over. Very much over.

• • • • • • • • • • • • • • • • • •

It's properly night by the time I reach the cottage. Dark windows. As I get near the door a feline shape slinks across the path, low and long and silent. Maybe that's what the underbelly's like – reserved for night, kept low to the ground. What could happen if you left it exposed? Right enough I've never seen the neighbours' cat roll onto her back, not even in the sun. Too much Siamese in her.

Fumbling for the light switch, there's a scuff of paper under my feet. Perhaps a job offer or an invitation for a free exotic holiday; a letter from a long-lost friend? A flair of light onto dusty quarry tiles and I blink at a bright green envelope. The words on it say 'The sensational mists of Victoria Falls', overlaid on a rainbow spray. 'Plus Free Postage and Packing.' Both somehow connected to an offer for the latest Next Directory. At least the people at Next know I exist. And the phone-line open until eleven pm if I need to chat to someone.

Not too late to phone Mary. The night bird. How does she manage to sound so sexy on her answerphone? Glasgow-husky, she's 'not available at present'. A series of beeps – she's been out for a while and had several calls. Or maybe out briefly but very popular? I leave a short message, forcing a sparkle into my voice. I once had a social life like that. Didn't I? Places to go. City life. Now scrape the odd evening out with nappy-centric mothers from work and into bed by ten pm. Still, moving to the country has its compensations – the seedlings in trays in the greenhouse, and walking around the flower beds on April evenings after work, seeing the first shoots in the cold earth.

And of course, I needed the change.

Coffee. Nut-brown and milky in my favourite porcelain cup. A treat. I hold it steady, snug in my cold hand. I inhale steam and coffee vapour and see the reflection of untidy hair and a shadeless bulb in the pool of coffee. Near the bottom, the caramel residue collects in one fine outer ring and in a central circle. Between the two, the cream base of the cup is flecked with grounds. I look closer for a meaning in their shape, trying to read them like tarot cards.

It reminds me of the bearded biker who read my cards for me in a pub once. He gave me a warning.

'You'll have to let it out, whatever it is. If you don't, there's going to be an almighty eruption! It'll come when you're least expecting it, when you're watching telly one night or something. Believe me ...' He looked at me sidelong at this point and I felt I had to control my smirk and make eye contact over the priestesses, hanged men, upside-down swords and my *n*th pint of cider. 'It happened to me.'

Really?

• • • • • • • • • • • • • • • • •

When I reach up to the shelf for the gin bottle, my hand brushes against a plain brown cardboard box. Quite small. Used to have some of my granny's silver in it; serviette rings and so on. It's propped among a clutter of vases, sewing things, and old Christmas cards. The clutter, within which my dreams lurk, like unread books.

I'm good at ignoring the box. I can keep it on the edge of my sight, just turn my head a little the other way to make it disappear. I developed this technique years ago in my bare flat in Manila to combat the tyranny of the cockroaches. When they made their presence felt with their whiskers and vile scuttlings, I just focused somewhere else. I didn't attack them with sprays or rolled up newspapers.

They simply weren't that important. Even when I crunched them under bare feet on my way to the loo at night, I didn't flinch, walked on, swept up the flat red shells in the morning.

The box is a bit like that. We cohabit uncomfortably. My relics box.

I open the lid cautiously. Nothing to fear. Half a dozen ageing items, fit for the bin. It's safe if I approach it with eyes only.

A cassette without a case. INXS. Not my choice. Not my cassette.

A champagne cork – still with its wee wire cage and silvery cap attached.

A fir cone.

A partly-used bottle of aftershave, Mostly Musk.

One purple sock.

Now with the box open on my lap, gin held tight, I'm conscious of my hand taking on a mind of its own. And it really is. It's tempted to take the lid off the aftershave and put the nozzle to my nose. With no thought to the consequences.

I put down my glass of gin.

· · · · · · · · · · · · · · · · · ·

The wheat field is luminous green in the morning-slanted sun. Even the plantation forest behind the cottage looks good today with its silver halo. Thank God for the relentless arrival of the next day.

In the car mirror, if I move my head a bit to the left, I can see my eyes. They look red, despite the heavy layer of mascara I've put on. Shadows underneath. Too late. Too much gin. Too stupid falling asleep on the sofa and waking up freezing at three am with the ribbed pattern of a sock imprinted on my face.

I take the roads easy this morning. In the daylight you can't tell if something's coming the other way. The bends now seem unexciting. I wave out of my rolled-down window at the postie, parked up in his red van beside Mrs Cameron's. He doesn't see me; head bent over important things on the passenger seat. Perhaps today's mail for me.

The suburbs. Roundabouts and greyish-brown council houses. A few people walk towards the centre. Men in suits carry their briefcases, heads alert to the sunshine. Even from the back I can picture them catching the eyes of the dog-walkers, joggers, women in overalls returning from early-morning cleaning jobs. Their half-smiles say 'what a beautiful day', 'I like you today.'

As I wait in the queue of traffic at the car park, I see a man in bottle-green overalls on the third floor of a building under construction. He's singing. Despite the engine noise, with the windows open and the sunshine-stillness of the air, the words are clear. He has a good voice. He swings his legs around an upright girder and, monkey-style, locks ankles and slides down to the next level. He continues to sing, the slightest jolt audible in his delivery of *Yellow Submarine* between floors. The man in the car next to me catches my eye and smiles. He has on a crisp white shirt and has nice lines around his eyes. I smile back. But I don't really see why I should, especially when he moves ahead faster than me in the queue.

Judy's already in the office, frowning at a computer screen. She's got shadows under her eyes too but to me her weariness has a sheen of domestic bliss.

'Hiyah! Gorgeous day.' I slip easily into my daytime persona. I picture it today as a yellow jump suit, following the shape of my body, but with enough slack in the fabric to disguise some of the imperfections underneath.

'Too nice to be in here. Should be in the garden.'

'Yep, I could be potting up my tomato seedlings, putting in the peas ...'

'I meant in the sun-lounger,' she says.

I laugh, flick on the kettle and sit down at my

desk. Two messages already. Must phone Beattie & Co. to check if the delivery's coming today.

'Hi, Sheila Armstrong here. Is that Karen? Gorgeous day isn't it?' I spin my chair to look at it through smoked glass fourth-floor windows. Mountains in the distance behind the dome of the City Hall. There's still a little snow on the peaks.

• • • • • • • • • • • • • • • • • •

Lunch-time in the High Street. I join the tightly packed group buzzing at the shelves in Di Marco's to get my filled croissant. Black grape and cambazola today. A bit more expensive than my usual cheddar and tomato, but I deserve a treat. I search for a drink on the refrigerator shelves. The radio blasts out a cheerful DJ, whose nonsense is probably fuelled by the solar euphoria that seems to have taken over the world today. During the first plucked chords, I move into the queue to pay. Then the singing starts. A Crowded House song: *Fall at Your Feet*.

Melodious and soft, it hooks in with no warning. My stomach lurches. I stand in the middle of the floor, bent slightly forward from the blow, croissant in its cellophane package in one hand and a carton of fresh orange in the other.

A malicious trick for this song to intrude now, to force a reaction. In daylight. Work hours. No alcohol involved. Perhaps it's the lack of sleep. I'm pushed out of the wings onto a stage, a world stage, with my relics box and a gin bottle. The underbelly exposed. Hideously caught out.

I crease forwards, becoming an angled, stick insect creature. The croissant hits the floor, bursting from its packaging. The two halves open like a shell, disgorging its innards. One rolling grape leaves a purple trail across the mock-marble floor. A foot in the queue steps back. Some of the soft croissant sticks to her heel when she moves forward again.

The song wails on.

'Sheila, are you not well?' Judy's at my side. I feel her tug at my elbow and her eyes searching my face. 'Are you all right?'

Of course. Of course I'm all right. It's just like the cockroaches. I just need to get a grip. 'I'll sweep it up,' I say. 'Don't worry, I'll sweep it up.'

'Come on,' Judy takes my arm. 'Let's go for a coffee.'

And she leads me out, away from the music, into a street which is blasted with midday sunlight. It illuminates every dark corner and alleyway.

The Glasshouse

'Come out for a drink. I'm going,' said Charlie, his blonde hair lifting from his head as if he'd been caught in a gust of wind.

'There's something on TV I want to watch.'

'Come on, you can't watch TV every night. You're turning into a couch potato.' He pushed fingers into Donna's stomach, but she brought up her hands and made a bony shield over her soft parts.

'My feet are too sore.'

He sighed, threw on his fleece and went to the door.

'Don't wake me up when you come in,' she said.

Donna's blisters had appeared after the night of the ceilidh. Maybe it was all the spinning on the balls of her feet; being too energetic to try and impress Charlie in the Gay Gordons. Or perhaps her feet had been sweaty – the wrong shoes; the wrong socks. He'd been radiant that night. The little laugh lines in the corners of his eyes never smoothed back to nonchalance the whole evening. She noticed it when she was sitting out a dance, cooling off, and he was stood opposite Kirsty waiting for the first chord of Strip the Willow, smiling with his eyes. That was when the blisters seemed to start.

On their doorstep afterwards she'd challenged him while she felt around in the gloom of her handbag for the key to the flat. 'She's attractive, yeah,' he'd said. 'Why? What's this about?' And then later on their domestic harmony had been shattered – they'd never fought like that before. She felt like Charlie had turned a light off, leaving her floundering in a darkened room.

Her feet were sore enough that she'd stayed in at night since then, putting them up on her homemade patchwork cushion on the arm of the sofa. She rubbed peppermint foot lotion into them, from the Body Shop. It made them tingle but did nothing to remove the blisters she could see deep and transparent beneath the tough skin. She wondered if she should pierce the skin with a sterilized needle to let the pus bubble out.

•   •   •   •   •   •   •   •   •   •   •   •   •   •   •   •

From the office window where she'd been working the last month, she could see most parts of the Victorian industrial site the men were restoring. The office was at the top of an old corn mill and had windows in all four walls. The men called it the watchtower, thinking that was where the management sat with their feet up all day watching the workers. Donna knew it wasn't really like that, although when the Boss was out of the room, she did sometimes sit and look through the window. Without moving from her desk she could see birds wheeling around in a big empty sky, and hills on all the edges of the panorama.

Watching work on the site was interesting too. She had to stand up and go to the window to see it properly. On hot days she got up from her desk when she heard the approach of the 'Mr Whippy' van through the neighbouring streets. The *Greensleeves* melody lurched off in mid-bar and peak-volume when the van stopped in the yard. She'd look down to see the cluster of men around it. They always seemed to be laughing and joking with each other – one of them would drop a chunk of strawberry Mivvi down another's shirt collar. She'd seen another one lick melted ice-cream from elbow to wrist, right through all the dust, when the others taunted him for not eating it quickly enough to stop the drips. The rooftop minstrels also drew her away from her desk. One of the men in particular sang quite well. She saw him often, straddling a roof ridge, with a hammer and a small radio which he accompanied at full volume.

She noticed that one of the men, the gardener,

Ron, kept himself a bit separate from the others. He worked alone, making beds and lawns out of several decades of rubble and wilderness. It was impressive, the transformation he'd created in a short time. There was a military touch to his garden – petunias pink, blue, pink, blue, left, right, left turn. A whole regiment of sunflowers against the wall didn't dare to stoop even when their heads got heavy with seeds. He was older than the other men and dressed differently, in head-to-toe combat gear, a pipe always clenched in the corner of his mouth.

Donna was growing herbs in the window box of the flat which she and Charlie had recently bought, so she could make them fresh salads in the evenings. She was developing an interest in gardening. Ron sometimes passed on tips to her, and he took her to see the seedboxes sprouting in the old glasshouse. They were screened from the harsher elements by huge slanting sheets of glass against the boiler house wall – this was where the restoration of the site had started.

'In the old days there'd have been cucumbers, tomatoes, the whole lot of them. Pity there's no heat from him in there no more.' He pointed with his pipe stem at the boiler-house wall. 'Have to rely on him.' Donna turned and screwed her eyes up at the ball of white sun piercing through the glass.

Ron was incomprehensible with his pipe in his mouth, but when he took it out, she saw the black teeth, and the smears around his mouth, as if he'd been eating liquorice. If she got too close, she could smell it too, stale on his breath. He was like some kind of pond-life.

When she first started the job, Donna noticed that Ron took his coffee break with the other men. They all dragged chairs out of the storeroom to sit in the sun. Ron sat solid and upright on the edge of the group, pouring orange squash from a khaki-covered canteen. The others lolled in a circle. After fifteen minutes, Ron stood up and packed his canvas knapsack back into the storeroom. He usually went straight back to his digging then, but one day she saw him stop and make some sort of speech to the other men. His pipe was clenched in his teeth, his hands on his hips. He seemed to be trying to wield some authority. None of them looked in his direction. He walked stiffly away, the pipe and his jaw set rigid together, and started digging over a new bed, kicking at the rocks. The other men shuffled back to their work ten minutes or so later. The Boss wasn't around that day.

Not long after that she started having to look out of a different window to see Ron having his coffee break, alone in the glasshouse.

• • • • • • • • • • • • • • • • • •

Donna always got back to the flat before Charlie. She put coffee on in the blackened espresso pot she'd brought back from Spain. She unscrewed the two parts of the pot, tapped the old grounds into the sink, filled it again and screwed it up ready to go on the hob. The ritual, with Radio 4 going in the background, was almost as comforting as actually drinking the coffee. She always had until at least *The Archers* before Charlie blew in, slapping a pile of newspapers onto the table and beginning his search for food. He was always ravenous by the time he came in. When they first moved in, she'd prepared a meal every evening to greet him, establishing a routine he'd never appeared to have before, and experimenting with recipes from the Sunday supplements. But since her feet had been so sore, she let him go back to ransacking the fridge when he came in, and then one of them would throw something together later in the evening. There was really no need to pamper him.

As the coffee prepared, she warmed a pan of milk. She heard the liquid spit its way into the upper chamber of the coffeepot. When she flipped the lid open to see how it was doing, she saw black slaps of coffee snorting through the tiny holes, and a dark caramel vapour pronged at her nostrils. While she was fiddling with the tuning on the radio, she heard the hiss as a volcano of frothing milk spilt and solidified onto the hob. 'Fuck you,' she said to the pan as it seethed back down at the flick of a switch. 'Bastard thing.' She stamped at the lino floor. Even inanimate objects were against her.

She ignored the mess and decided to drink the coffee black. She took down a tin from the shelf above the cooker and clinked two brown sugar cubes into the cup before she poured the spitting coffee onto them. When she put the spoon in to stir, she found nothing of the cubes left. It reminded her of a science experiment she'd done at school with one of her discarded milk teeth and an egg-cup of Coca-Cola. After a month, that small hard part of her was completely gone. It seemed almost impossible, that such hard things could be dissolved clean away.

She was dozing when Charlie came in, her feet throbbing and raised on the arm of the sofa. He woke her by putting a hand on them, making her jump.

'Get off. They're sore.' The shock caught her, still vulnerable in sleep, so her words came out in a sort of sob.

'Hey, puss, what's up?'

Donna rubbed her eyes, bent her knees so her feet were as far from him as possible. 'Must've fallen asleep.'

He put a hand on the top of one foot and stroked down the slope of bone from ankle to toe. 'What's with the feet?'

She looked down, but she was still blurry with sleep – a black blot in her vision where her feet should have been. 'Nothing. They're just sore.'

'Poor things.' He patted her feet. 'They take something like five hundred tons of force every day, you know.' Then he got up to turn the TV on, using the remote to turn the volume right down so they could still hear *The*

Archers. He always created this kind of chaos when he came in, always had to have every sort of stimulus.

She tucked her feet up beside her, rolling the soles up so that she could see the blisters still there under the gnarled skin.

•   •   •   •   •   •   •   •   •   •   •   •   •   •   •   •   •

From the office window she could see the stream burbling through the gardens that Ron was creating. It sparkled and danced at the bottom of a steep channel, apparently content despite surrendering half its flow to heave the rusty old water wheel around. She'd been pulled to the window by raised voices in the garden. She recognized Ron's voice. It echoed right across the site like the bellow of a monster with an arrow stuck in its hide, furious at the knowledge it's going to die. As she got to the window, she saw Ron running beside the stream, his stiff legs lurching him from side to side at the hips. As he ran, he looked into the stream, and he tripped over steps and rocks and gravel, his arms windmilling to keep him in balance. The other men were upstream, thermoses and hard hats at their feet, a cement mixer churning behind them. She saw hands raising dust as they slapped onto thighs, one of the men so doubled by laughter that he sank to his knees, his face screwed up, gasping for breath.

Ron threw himself down the steps into the stream bed. Wading knee-deep in the water, he slipped and stumbled over greasy rocks before lunging at the water, straightening up when he caught something. He tapped it against the wall of the channel. It was his pipe. He peered into it, tapped it again, and she saw a small ball of something grey plop out of it into the water near his feet. He planted the pipe back into his mouth and heaved himself back up the steps, water squirting out of the tops of his black army boots.

He ignored the other men who were now shuffling with their cups and sandwich boxes and walked slowly across the garden to where the Boss stood with his hands on his hips. After a brief exchange, in which Ron's hand trembled, pointed, and fell back to his pipe, he walked away. She saw the Boss walk towards the group of men. It was then that she guessed the grey ball in the pipe had been cement. She returned to her desk in case they looked up and saw her. She wasn't shirking, but she would hate anyone to think she was. Sometimes it seemed like it was only she and Ron that got on with their jobs without time wasting.

The phone rang all afternoon. Builders' merchants; the architect; an industrial archaeologist. She could see the Boss out in the yard, sharing a joke with some of the men, evidently complacent about what they'd done to Ron. He wasn't available to come and answer all the phone enquiries. If she'd had a minute, she would have phoned Charlie to moan about it. All the annoyance seemed to make her feet sorer, and when the Boss came back into the office, she had to quickly pull them off a seat, and slot them back into her shoes.

• • • • • • • • • • • • • • • • • •

When Donna woke up the next morning, she searched around for a fragment of dream that was bothering her. It returned while she was sitting on the floor sticking Compeed plasters onto the soles of her feet. Ron, suspended in the air, each of his four limbs in the clutches of one of the labourers. They stretched his body between them. On the instructions of the fifth man, conducting from the sidelines – 'one, two, three, PULL!' – they strained him further. It was like young boys pulling the legs off spiders. Ron made no sound. But the arch of his back, the bucking of his chest, the pipe clamped vertical, the eyes staring, said it all. He was wild.

'Let me look.' Charlie knelt on the floor next to her, lifted up one of her feet and inspected the blistered ball of it. Then he kissed it. 'There. Better now?'

'It tickles,' she said, pulling her foot away from him. She pulled on her socks and stood up, ready to go to work. The dream still tugged at her, some remaining detail she hadn't recaptured. She wondered whether, under his thick leather boots, Ron had blisters too, eating a dark channel up towards his knees from the soles of his feet. Perhaps she had known this in the dream?

'I'll be late tonight,' Charlie said.

'Oh?'

'Football, remember. And then maybe a drink.'

Who with? she wondered. His life seemed such a breeze, while the atmosphere seemed to push her down towards the centre of the earth, the weight pressing entirely through the soles of her feet. It wasn't fair. She'd put so much effort into building their life together – the flat, the window boxes, the choice of groceries. He just floated about enjoying himself. He might as well have been pulling her into pieces like the labourers and Ron in her dream.

•   •   •   •   •   •   •   •   •   •   •   •   •   •   •   •   •   •

It was another fine summer morning and Donna took her coffee outside, wandering through the garden with her mug. She sat down to take the weight off her feet, and watched the ducks in the stream.

'Lovely day, hen,' Ron paused his wheelbarrow, the sun behind him.

She shaded her eyes with one hand and looked into his shadow. 'The garden's looking great, Ron.'

'Coming on, coming on. Lupins'll be out soon.' He pointed his pipe to the bed next to her. 'Just need to keep the weeds down, keep the slugs off.' He pulled a plastic tub out of his jacket pocket and rattled it. 'These'll get the blighters.'

'Isn't there a kinder way?' she asked. She'd seen the explosions of gunge that were once slugs scattered around the garden, smearing their death throes in a sheen across cement paths.

'What do you want to feel sorry for slugs for?' His pipe wiggled in his mouth as he laughed. 'Kill 'em dead, that's what I say. Firing squad. No mercy.'

As they laughed together, she heard the first line of a song rise from one of the rooftops behind her. A hammer provided the beat. 'Daisy, daisy, give me your answer, do.' In reply from the another roof came 'I'm half crazy ...' followed by a wild howl. After a pause for thought the first voice warbled. Then a tuneless shriek shot up from the yard somewhere. 'Roses are red, violets are blue,' and the rooftop answered 'Planted by a fucker with a didgeridoo.' Laughter bellied up from all corners of the site.

Ron shuffled his feet and muttered something through his pipe she couldn't understand. He bristled back to the wheelbarrow and plodded away with it towards the shield of the glasshouse. He wasn't going to see any funny side.

It was later the same day as she sat with her feet up in the office again, that she heard a splintering sound below, followed by shouting. She rushed to the window, shoeless, to see an axe head crashing through the closed storeroom door from the inside. It scattered the group of labourers standing around outside it. She watched as a rough hole began to appear near the door handle. Then the Boss was there, spinning around the semi-circle of men in a flurry of questions. The men's heads were bowed, denying all. She saw him bang his hand on what was left of the door and turn the key. He was swept backwards with the hinges as Ron's figure erupted from inside, the axe held above his head, hobbling towards the men. Donna envisaged the roar as he swung the axe down, missing the scattering men and embedding it in the tarmac instead.

Then he yanked it up again and flailed away, wading into the centre of one of his floral beds. He raised the axe and slashed it down through the lupins, lopping off the promise of their flower heads. He swirled it around his ankles and swept the heads off the dahlias, stamping on the surviving foliage. Then he kicked his way through the long bed of petunias beside the stream, booting them to death with the energy of a small boy in autumn leaves. When he reached the end of the bed, he didn't turn left. He jerked himself onto the path, and stalked towards the glasshouse, still gripping the axe.

'No,' she said to herself. She flung open the window and shouted after him, 'Ron!' But he didn't hear her. She couldn't bear to see him destroy everything, all his hard work. She grabbed her shoes and ran down the stairs, chasing across the grass to try and stop his madness. She had no doubt he was going to take it out on the glasshouse. The thing he was most proud of with its clean new sheets of glass pouring light and warmth onto his seedlings. She steeled herself for the first rings of shattering glass.

As she turned the corner of the boiler house, she saw Ron's back, stopped on the path, and his shoulders grasped between the Boss's hands. They were nose to nose. The hands and shoulders rose and fell with Ron's breathing. Donna imagined the fug of breath they must be enveloped in.

When she got back to her tower, she saw the Boss release Ron's shoulders, turning him back towards the storeroom. He came out with the canvas knapsack on his back and lifted a stiff leg over his bicycle. She watched him wobble out through the gate.

• • • • • • • • • • • • • • • • • •

Donna didn't feel like coffee when she got home that night. She needed something lighter, more cleansing. She ended up with a mug of boiled water which tasted surprisingly good although she missed the pleasure of the coffee-making ritual.

Charlie came in and sat by her feet at the end of the sofa as she rested with her eyes closed.

'How was your day?' she asked.

'Oh, you know, the usual. Yours?'

'*Un*usual.'

'Yeah?'

'A mad axe-man on the premises.'

'We've got one of those too. The financial manager.'

'A bit more literal this one.'

'Did he behead anyone?'

'Only the flowers he's spent the last six months raising on tender loving care. He was like a monster. And to think I was feeling sorry for him because he got treated so badly.' She pictured the devastated flowerbeds and shivered at the waste, the ruin. The work of an angry man intent on destroying himself.

Charlie stroked the tops of her feet and she looked up at him. She felt his reassuring weight next to her on the sofa and recognized the smile he had for her in his laugh lines. She got up to open a window, allowing a warm breeze to curl in a wheel around the room. When she sat back down she stretched her feet onto Charlie's lap.

'Give them a massage,' she said. She'd forgotten how good he was at massage, how sensitive. She felt a lightening in her spine, a stretching upwards. When he started to rub into the sole with his thumbs, she didn't pull her foot away. The strength of sensation she'd become used to in her feet transformed from pain and throbbing into warmth. It was as if the water she was drinking was dissolving the bubbles under the skin away, easing out the fluid. She closed her eyes again, drifted towards sleep.

'You know what?' Charlie had stopped massaging and was frowning at the sole of her foot. 'It's going. Your blister. It's got smaller.' He picked up the other foot. 'And that one.'

Through the drift and drowse she opened her eyes slightly and looked towards her feet. She couldn't see them at all – just a ball of soft light into which her feet and Charlie's hands melted.

Eye to Eye

The cat's eyes and white lines beat beneath me. Hypnotize.
And on the periphery of the road, I'm aware of the longer
pulse of telegraph poles, the quick flicker of fence posts,
and the soft fall of dusk light on conifer branches. I see
nothing beyond this, not at this speed. I power into the
corners now I've regained my confidence on the un-
seasonally dry tarmac.

It's that time of year when the bikes reclaim the
roads. A day that tricks you with its warmth. It lures you out
to flash in the sunlight the chrome and paint work you've
been polishing in the garage all winter. But it's not spring
yet, not really. When you're way out of the city, the cold
claws in with the dusk. It dulls the euphoria a bit. But you're
committed; too far to turn back. Cold wraps around you,
sinks its teeth into your joints. The knees; especially the
knees.

• • • • • • • • • • • • • • • • • •

'You're just like a wee boy,' she said when I decided to go on
the bike.

'C'mon Carol, where's your sense of fun?'

'Fun?' The way she stared at me cut into my
excitement. 'He's dying, Martin.'

I looked up from cleaning last year's flies off my
helmet visor. 'And how many times has he been "dying"
before?' She knew I was right when I looked back at her
silence. 'This isn't the first time I've done the Highland
Dash, you know. And it's the quickest way.'

'Oh, aye, it's your eagerness to get to the sick bed
that's squeezed you into your leathers, is it?'

'It'll give him a kick if I go on the bike, too. You
wait – he'll be riding pillion in his pyjamas.' She looked at
me in that way again. 'You know what he's like Carol, the

guy's indestructible.'

'That's the dishcloth you're turning into an insect mortuary, by the way.' She grabbed it out of my hand and started wiping around the sink. I picked up the boots I'd bought in the winter sales and blew dust off them. Reinforced and leather lined. At last a chance to road test them.

'That's an end to me coming with you then,' she said. 'You needn't think I'm going to perch on the back of that thing freezing my butt off for hours on end.'

'You've got things to do here anyway, yeah?' I put the boots down and placed my hands on her shoulders; forced some eye contact. It was a pity she was being such a cow. The March sunlight blew in the cherry blossom on the drying green and speckled in through the kitchen window. Her hair glowed, tied up in a blue scarf, and her neck seemed to stretch in the warmth. 'You don't really want to be bothered with my old Dad, do you?'

She turned away from me a little, then looked sideways at me, one blue eye hard and unblinking.

'Just bugger off and get going; it'll be cold later.'

I kissed her. She didn't understand.

• • • • • • • • • • • • • • • • • •

The loch next to the road catches the final evening light. I used to know this stretch intimately – every bend and pothole, where the patches of gravel were likely to send your tyres sliding. Us boys, we'd come over here after the pub on a Saturday night. Sometimes in the Summer we'd stop and jump in the loch fully clothed, light a fire to sit around for a bit and then back on the bikes down to the village, freezing cold, dawn coming. Would I go faster or slower now? I've got more power – nine hundred cc to the two-fifty then. But in those days we had no doubts. Until Jamie got wiped out by a tourist caravan wandering into his lane. That pulled us up for a while. Somewhere around here, the bend. This time of year the daffodils his family planted come up; a touch of gardener's love in a desert of heather. After that Mum turned away when she saw me come down the stairs in my leathers. Waited by the door to meet me when she heard the bike coming down the brae. I don't remember where Dad was.

There's car tail-lights ahead of me now, the first for ages. They blink visible and invisible around the bends on the rise ahead. I'll be on them soon. It still gives me a kick to roar up behind and brake slightly behind their bumper, waiting for the space ahead. I imagine their anxious eyes in the rear-view mirror, watching my hands black on the bars and the headlight burning in. Then I drop a couple of gears, flick out to skim the driver side, accelerate hard away. Sometimes you can do it all so quickly the car seems to travel backwards.

There's just the final summit to go now before the brae down to the village. The sky's big above me. The land falls grey and shadowless away from the sunken sun. My headlight forges across the moor, the angulation of red and white snow poles beckoning me forward. There's distant orange lights below and silence beyond the engine growl. The cold's deep in my hands. They'll be agony when I stop and the blood returns, but I don't feel it yet.

Now I'm on the top; high and alone and that left-hander must be soon. The one I used to be able to take at seventy if I got the bend right. Get onto the white line, or further right at night when you could tell nothing was coming the other way. Then drop onto the left wall of your tyres, going for the glory of sparks from your metal toe protectors. The smooth acceleration, pulling upright as the view down the glen appears. The 'home bend' we called it.

And here it comes – there's the flicker of white chevron ahead. But my focus jumps as something whiter catapults out from the verge ahead. One. Two. Three. The white mountain hares hang, strobe-struck in the headlight. The first leaps an impossible span; the second triangles –

back legs overtaking front; the last launches upwards from the iron spring of back legs. Pink-eyed, they play their game of chance. They breach the road, impossibly close, impossible to miss. I close my eyes.

•　•　•　•　•　•　•　•　•　•　•　•　•　•　•　•　•

As I pass the village sign, I drop my speed, sit up a bit as the rush of wind through my helmet eases. I pull up my visor. The peat smoke tickles my nostrils, tells me I'm home. I hear the engine and enjoy the luxury of seeing beyond the road. The petrol station, stripped of pumps; The Crown, a curtain tugged across lit windows; smoke reaching upwards from the cottage chimneys into a clear sky. And as I turn into the lane, follow the terrace down, the silhouette of my mother is in the backlit square of doorway, one hand on the door frame. Her face is black, blank.

I kill the engine. The silence shocks my ears and brings a warmth – the successful completion of an adventure; the return journey to my youth. I swing my right leg over the seat and ease myself straight. She's still standing in the doorway, doesn't come out. She always did that, as if by coming outside she'd transgress into the male world of engine rebuilds on the drive and what she called Dad's 'bits of wood' in the garage. Tonight the garage door is firmly closed. He started years back making furniture and ornaments out of cast-off timber, but he got really keen after his retirement. The house is full of stools with legs of uneven length and clocks with enormous plywood hands which Mum hides when visitors come.

The detail of her silhouette doesn't fill out until I'm almost at the door. She takes a small step back and the kitchen strip-light bares all on her face. The smile doesn't reach her eyes.

'How're you doing, Mum?'

'Mart … I tried to phone but Carol said you'd already left – no way to contact you.'

I feel my face flush with guilt-blood – perhaps the concentration, or the brain subdued with cold – I'd more or less forgotten until this moment why I'm here. We move fully into the kitchen light and close the door. I pull the helmet off with one hand, the other arm still cupped across my front. 'What's happened?' I put the helmet down on the Formica top.

'He was taken worse. The doctor came. Said he should go into hospital. An ambulance came.' I put a hand out, touch her shoulder. My expectations evaporate. The muffled greeting from his armchair in front of the TV, or from his pillow, next to a pile of magazines, bottles of pills and Irn Bru. I'd taken it for granted they'd be there as usual. The enjoyment of my journey fades. No longer a heroic return.

I realize how cold I am, go across to lean against the Rayburn which throws a lifeline of heat to me. Pots and plates on its shiny black top promise a hot meal. The blood starts to circulate.

'What will they do for him there?'

'They said he was dehydrated, needed to be on a drip. He hasn't eaten the last few days – couldn't keep anything down.'

'He's conscious, though, yeah?'

She nodded. 'But confused, weak.' One of her hands clutches a handkerchief, screwed into a ball as both hands clamp her upper arms. I've never seen her look so small.

'Sounds like he's in the best place, Mum. We'll go and see him in the morning.' I search for some consolation for us both, for the strangeness of his absence. 'I'll take you on the bike.'

She manages a small hiccupy laugh. Now my hands are throbbing and I press them one at a time under the opposite armpit, the other hand staying across my belly. I jiggle my feet to take my mind off the pain.

'Have you got a cardboard box, Mum?'

'Why?'

'I'll show you.'

While she goes to look for one, I start to undo the zip of my leather jacket. I pull it out and away from me, stopping once the white head is exposed. The nose is curled downwards, the long ears pressed back against the head and neck. I stroke the hard top of its head with a finger.

'What have you got there?' she asks, coming back in with a box.

'A hare, Mum. I hit it on the top road there. Think its back legs are broken.'

'Oh for goodness sake.' She rises on her toes to look into the top of my jacket. The one exposed eye rolls and blinks. 'It'll just die of shock won't it?'

'I could hardly leave it there, Mum. He was dragging himself around on the road.'

She sighs and puts the box on the floor in front of the Rayburn.

'If he survives the night, I'll take him down to the vet's tomorrow, see if they can get a splint on the legs.'

I press the body to my chest with one hand and undo the jacket zip completely with the other. Despite the appearance of size created by his thick coat, my hand compresses onto slight bones.

'Here, put this in first.' She puts an old gardening jumper of Dad's into the box. The hare struggles a bit as I cradle him in, his front legs pushing against my arm. But the back legs trail, ridiculously long. Once he's in the box he stops moving. All except the eye.

•   •   •   •   •   •   •   •   •   •   •   •   •   •   •   •   •   •

In some sense, Dad not being there makes the evening a special occasion. The usual routine of my visits home goes out the window. We don't watch TV, Mum doesn't fuss with trays and walking sticks, and she doesn't have to retire to the washing-up when we start on about the bike and the latest in piston rings and shock absorbers. She and I stay in the kitchen, spend the evening sat on either side of the hare in his box. My head and body still feel the throb of the road. We look down at him and his eye, offer him saucers of milk and bits of carrot which he doesn't take. We stay up later than usual, discuss Dad's return from hospital. I offer to move his bed into the sitting room to make it easier for them. We agree to phone the hospital first thing in the morning and then take the bus into town, to see him.

'Aren't you supposed to put a lid on – keep him in the dark?' she says when we're about to go to bed.

'I don't know, Mum.'

'Remember that time your Dad brought back an owl?' She's quiet a minute and then laughs. 'He put a lid on but he took it off every half-hour to have a peek. In the end it had enough, started flapping around the kitchen with the three of us and the cat chasing it. Remember?' We laugh.

She folds a blanket and goes to put it over the box. 'Never realized they were so big – such beautiful fur.' And she touches it with the knuckle of her handkerchief hand. She whispers, 'It's OK, my pet, you get some rest.'

As I get into bed I imagine Dad supported in through the door by ambulance men, to find a beautiful white hare recovering in his kitchen. I reckon he'll be pleased. But then it occurs to me. I'm assuming he will be coming back from hospital.

• • • • • • • • • • • • • • • • •

I wake in the morning with instant apprehension. What's happened in the night? I go straight down to the kitchen in my pyjamas without dressing. Up before Mum, like a wee boy again with Christmas presents to open or exam results arriving in the post. But I don't recall this fear. The blanket is still in place. I lift it a little and see the eye. It's open. I pull the blanket off. The eye stays open for too long.

Unblinking. I put my hand against the shoulder, onto the wide padded paw. Cold. Mum comes into the room behind me and I turn to see her tying her dressing gown belt.

'He's dead.'

She doesn't speak for a moment, frowns towards the box.

'I'm going to phone the hospital,' she says and leaves the room.

Kneeling on the floor, I lift the cold hare out of the box, lay him across my thighs. The coat seems rougher now without the oily warmth from the skin. From the hall I can hear Mum's voice on the phone. I can't make out the words and the tone gives nothing away. The house empties; empties of recovering animals, carburettors in small pieces on newspaper in the kitchen, new wooden monstrosities to learn to live with. As if something's sucked every last bit of his influence out though the windows, the house empties of Dad. I put the hare back in his box and go to get dressed. The eye stares up at me.

Advent

After I'd settled into the hotel room, unpacking my spongebag, hanging up suits and blouses in the wardrobe, and plugging in the laptop ready for the inevitable evening's work, I took the advent calendar Malcolm had given me out of a large envelope. I re-opened the three windows which had been squashed flat, and stood it on the desk.

We don't make a fuss about Christmas, usually both work flat out until the last minute, then treat it as a long weekend. The advent calendar was a first that year, because I was going to be away from home. I wasn't sure that I liked the gesture – was it so I could count the days until we were back together? Or was he seriously suggesting I should get worked up about Christmas?

'It's definite,' I'd said, 'I'm to spend two weeks at the Head Office.'

'OK. Why's that again?'

'To work with the editorial team there. It's a new series of Maths books. For secondary schools.'

'Interesting?'

'Not specially.'

He was organizing papers for the next day's meetings at one end of the sofa. My briefcase spilled open at my feet at the other.

'You'll miss my office dinner dance,' he said, putting a sheaf of papers back into a folder.

'Yes.' Indifference sat between us like an adolescent at a grown-up party. 'Well, never mind, all that dressing up stuff, champagne and smoochy dancing aren't really my thing.'

•   •   •   •   •   •   •   •   •   •   •   •   •   •   •   •

On the first morning at the hotel, before leaving for the office, I sat down at the desk and dutifully opened the fourth window on the calendar. It felt vaguely familiar: the anticipation as I scanned for the next number amongst the menagerie of reindeers, robins and angels; the graze of glitter against my finger; and finally, the unlocking of a miniature revelation by a fingernail hooked under a flap in the card. That day the window revealed a parcel, wrapped around with a large yellow ribbon.

The walk to the office gave me a new vision of the midwinter city. The whole population seemed to have come out in the middle of the night and vomited on the pavements. Sometimes only dark star-shaped stains were left by the pigeons. Cars were made foolish with traffic cones on their roofs. Streamers, tinsel and deflated balloons dangled from benches and telephone boxes.

I left the office for a breath of fresh air at lunch-time and found the morning quiet had surrendered to clamour, as workers emptied offices to take over restaurants. Cars circulated the city with tinsel streaming from their aerials, bass beats bulging their windows outwards. I couldn't make out how anyone got any work done. I felt misplaced, frumpy in office clothes, in the midst of a massive street party.

Leaving the office under cover of darkness at five o'clock, I shared the pavements with shoppers and party-goers. Groups of young people with arms locked shouted Christmas pop songs. After midnight as I packed up the laptop, I could see from my hotel window men in suits and dark overcoats weaving along pavements, briefcases still clutched under their arms. They bantered with groups of girls on their way to clubs. I wondered if they had wives who had to put up with their cold bodies crashing late into bed and snoring.

• • • • • • • • • • • • • • • • •

By the time I got to opening the ninth window of the advent calendar, I found myself looking forward to it. My morning search and discovery was becoming an enjoyable ritual. The sprig of mistletoe gave me a little glow of surprise. It would give me something to report to Malcolm when I phoned him later.

Towards the end of a meeting that day, my colleagues started talking about a job which had nothing to do with me; the details of some book promotion which would happen when I was weeks away from there. My mind started to wander, but I positioned my features and the angle of my head to look attentive, moved my eyes onto whoever was speaking. The occasional nod or murmur. Terry was in full flood, a cigarette stubbed out in front of him, black coffee half drunk, saying something about post-modernism.

The game started because as I watched he took his jacket off, hooked it over the back of the chair; never stopped talking. I continued the process. Cream polo neck slipped easily over his arms and head; slip-on shoes slipped off; olive green chinos dropped to his ankles; and finally the underwear (vest, no; boxers, yes). I kept it decent, snipped the elastic hospital-style with scissors and kept my eyes averted. Then I scooped him up in my forearms, and laid him gently into a satin-lined coffin, pressed his eyelids down with my thumbs. He immediately became inoffensive. In fact, mysteriously, I warmed to him. I obscured the chuckle which was threatening to escape in a cough. Margaret was flashing her gold earrings and long red nails – she could be next.

Once I'd laid them all out, I found myself returning to Terry. Something was missing. That was it – today's advent image. I put a spray of mistletoe between the clasped hands on his chest. He was ready for action. What would his beyond-the-grave kisses be like I wondered – warm or cold? Then I realized eyes were on me, looking for an answer to something. I felt a blush burn against my collar.

•   •   •   •   •   •   •   •   •   •   •   •   •   •   •   •   •   •   •

As December progressed, meetings frequently finished with an invitation for lunch. At first I tried to escape, clutching my briefcase, but the atmosphere was persuasive. Normally stressed-out editors smiled more, gave in to this pressure with weary fatalism. My office routines were over a hundred miles away. Barmen tempted us with mulled wine or cocktails. No one cared about big bar bills. Christmas pop played in the background. I found myself drawn into conversations about families and friends, not about work. The boundaries between work and pleasure seemed to blur.

The office night-out came around. Between leaving work and meeting the others at the restaurant, I had about two and a half hours and I wasn't going to sit at my laptop. It was dark, and as I strolled up the hill, briefcase in gloved hand, I could see through the windows that the bars were already filling up. My breath misted out in front of my face, fogged the milky way of lights suspended from trees along the High Street.

In front of me a girl emerged out of a pub and swung around to laugh back in through the door. Music and laughter escaped onto the pavement for a moment before the door enclosed the party again. The girl turned and walked up the street ahead of me, lighting a cigarette. A white wool jacket swung around her hips, accentuated the long legs in black velvet jeans. Her dark hair was cut sharp at her shoulders; it shone and swung under the streetlights.

It was Thursday – the shops stayed open late. A thought occurred to me. I could buy something special to wear, before a quick shower at the hotel. A present to myself. I wandered into the shopping centre, brushing against groups of teenage girls who glowed and bounced in short-skirted clusters, geared up with carrier bags from Oasis, rolls of wrapping paper and wide smiles. I found a shop I didn't know; not one I frequent for my publishing executive clothes. Soul music slunk around it, removed workday worries, suggested a different order of priorities; the importance of partying and the need to glitter. I avoided the obvious festive clothes – too transparent, skimpy, black. I could imagine what Malcolm would say, 'You're not in your twenties now, Fiona!'

It was the feel that sold the blouse to me. My fingers strayed onto it when I was looking at something on the next hanger. It poured against my hand like oil. I expected black or chocolate brown, and was surprised by deep orange.

V-necked and long-sleeved, it was cut in at the waist and then flared out. I faced the mirror in the fitting room as I buttoned it up, feeling the velvet slip and warm against the skin of my waist. As I moved to look from the side, the velvet hem swung heavily, as the white coat on the girl earlier had done. I found myself smiling into the mirror, pulled my hair up and off my face, twisted it on the top of my head, and looked again. Something was coiled up in my stomach. Excitement. It was how Christmas felt when I was a child.

•   •   •   •   •   •   •   •   •   •   •   •   •   •   •   •   •   •

To get into the club, we had to push between bodies melted together by the crowd. Bare shoulders glowed in the lowlight. It was hot, and I felt over-dressed in the black crombie which had barely kept me warm in the sharpness of the street. The volume of the music and the crush conspired to make everyone intimate, forcing heads together, brushing lips on ears for the simplest conversation about orders at the bar. The coil in my stomach seemed to compress and expand, resonating with the beat of the music. The pressure of bodies, the heat, the unfamiliarity, all added to it. Imagine ever doing this at home. It was better not to think of that.

I'd already drunk more than I was used to, but I wanted more. We dazzled smiles at each other. I was left alone with the afterglow as Margaret went for drinks and Terry took away the coats. Aware of the way the light hit the orange blouse, I dropped my shoulders, laughed upwards, felt the heavy velvet swing.

From the direction of the cloakroom, a sprig of mistletoe advanced. Trembling above heads, it pitched and stalled its way towards me.

'Happy Christmas!' Terry darkened my space with an arm around my shoulder, caught the edge of my mouth with a kiss which smelt of warm leather, and tasted faintly of smoke. It should have been disgusting. A gurgle of laughter bubbled up from the bottom of my stomach. I felt the curl of orange around me, felt my whole body smile. It was so completely what I deserved. Like Belgian chocolates after a heavy week of meetings. It was familiar. As if I was in a film. Emulating black-and-white, Ingrid Bergman glamour. As he pulled away to continue his mistletoe pilgrimage, he slurred 'sexy stuff' and rubbed a bit of my sleeve between his fingers. And I knew, absolutely, that I was desirable.

• • • • • • • • • • • • • • • • • •

In the narrow street on the way back to the hotel, I followed a young man with a ponytail. His leather trousers were well fitting, slightly ruckled around the ankles, his legs bowed a little at the knee, enough to suggest athleticism. He turned his head a little, in a vulnerable way, aware of my presence behind him. If I could whistle, I might have been tempted to.

Back in the hotel room my ears buzzed and I didn't feel like sleep. I sat on the edge of the bed and looked at the few things I had to pack. I picked up the advent calendar, looked at the pictures of parcels and mistletoe, the white-bearded man assuring happiness. Only a few windows to go. It was nice of Malcolm to give it to me. It had been fun. It had gained a special status, but that had nothing to do with being away from or going back to Malcolm. It was as if it marked a time in which I'd been allowed to play, to enjoy some midwinter madness. I put my lips to it, pushed the windows shut and put it back into the envelope, ready to go in my suitcase.

And then I recognized a new feeling. Not the coil in my stomach this time, but another of those feelings from Christmases past. Usually it comes a bit later though, on Christmas Day, when you're searching around under heaps of torn wrapping paper, and you realize there are no presents left to undo.

I took the new blouse off, pressed my nose deep into its smoothness. Breathed in smoke, beer, a faint whiff of aftershave. I put it on a hanger by the window to air, opened the empty suitcase on the bed, and went over to the wardrobe. I decided on a navy suit for the journey home, and started to fold all the other clothes into the case. A thought flirted its way into my mind, shameless and brazen. It danced across in front of me as I leant over the suitcase, flattening the pleats of a skirt. I looked over one shoulder at the navy suit, and over the other at the orange blouse. They both hung there, suspended above the floor, watching me like a couple of angels. All they needed was wings. I stood up and smiled at the navy suit as I pulled it off its perch and stuffed it into the suitcase. I'd wear the orange blouse home. Smells and all.

The Craftsman

Our gaze gets disconnected by the coach moving forward. Her chestnut hair swings over her shoulder as she turns to face the front. She reaches down, perhaps for her bag on the floor. I can almost sense that secret nobble at the top of her spine, the one I want to touch, to curl my body against. And I feel the after-burn of her gaze. It would be fun to catch that smile, and hear that giggle again.

• • • • • • • • • • • • • • • • •

Eyes on me. Like magnets they spin my head around to meet them, across a road and through a pane of City Link glass. The coach vibrates blue and yellow at the lights on Renfield Street, on its way out of town from the Bus Station. And, fuck me, if they're not eyes I know. Or knew. Her eyes. It all happens so quick I feel caught out, on the pavement adjusting my belt, no idea I was on show. The shock throws me onto my back in a room with pink curtains drawn against summer evening light and our stomachs slipping against each other warm with massage oil and sweat. Even that smell, of the oil, sweet and hippyish, is with me right now. I put my shopping down on the pavement, a bit behind me, a bit out of sight.

How long is it since I've seen her – maybe four of five years? She just disappeared, out of sight, out of mind, like a heavy pebble tossed into the Clyde. A few ripples right enough. Women don't go without a few ripples. She moved down to Ayrshire so I heard. That's why I never run into her I suppose. She might even be married now, with children.

She doesn't look away. But she's not waving or smiling either. She hated me at the end. Angry about something I didn't understand. She phoned a few times, her voice on the other end tense like an over-inflated balloon, saying she 'had-to-know-why', 'needed-to-understand', 'couldn't cope'. The usual things. I was patient, talked her through it, even when I had my coat on ready to go out. By the end of our chat, she was calmer, even managed a bit of a laugh. We were always good at sharing a joke. And I'd put down the phone and go down the pub with the boys, or raise an eyebrow with the pal who'd been waiting for me all that time. More women trouble, eh? They were used to it.

My hands are firmly by my sides; my face not showing anything yet, like hers. Now I'm feeling a bit less shaky, after the suddenness of it, shouldn't I acknowledge her? I mean, she's staring straight at me. Full fucking frontal I am, on the pavement, waiting to cross the road and I'm just seeing a tiny part of her. She's visible only from the chin upwards – above the window height of the coach. Which is funny because my image of her was somehow always the opposite; from the neck downwards. The head and face were the bits I felt least intimate with. Maybe it was all those times from behind, faceless, how I liked it best. And the time I could never forget, when she straddled me in the car outside the cinema. Her face was masked from the car park lights by her hair flopping forwards. Could have been a stranger. Even when we were face to face I don't remember taking much notice. Just the hair, her long hair that I could pin to the pillow with my fists. I loved that feeling of tautness; knowing she couldn't move. Brilliant that was.

There was a place I loved on her. A nobble at the top of her spine. The best thing was touching it secretly, under her hair, when we were out. It turned us both on. My finger running over the nobble, the slight hardness under the slide of skin. Christ, I wanted to fuck her brains out. We went to places where there was a crowd on purpose. Foreplay. The music and all the folk pressed our hips and thighs together more and more as the evening wore on. It was hard to hang on there, not to scoot straight off to her place, practically tearing each other's clothes off in the cab. Even now the thought of it sends a shiver down my belly. There was no denying the spark. Her legs used to stick to me with sweat, wrap around me so strongly I sometimes felt she was going to suck me into her, like I was in a trap. One of those female spiders who eat their mate after they've performed. Some thanks.

Perhaps it was only a good fuck she wanted anyway. I had that feeling in the early days. I thought she might have been taking the piss – bragging to her university friends about her 'bit of rough'. It threw me a bit at first. Sex, women; it's a game, right? A bit like alien invaders. You blow one up and then the next one comes along. I'd always felt pretty sure of that. I didn't like the thought I might be part of *her* game. But she soon fell for me. I realized she was keen pretty early on. Walking down the dark street I saw her appear at the tenement window. She was a silhouette in a triangle of light swished open by the curtain. There was an arm pulling across it, and a dark face searching the street. She was waiting for me, gagging for it. That put a wee bounce in my step.

There was a TV programme around the time we started seeing each other. It always seemed to be on when I got to her place. A documentary about the Arctic, or the Antarctic maybe – *Life in the Freezer*. We always watched it before we went out. I remember the bit when David Attenborough was wading through a beachful of elephant seals. Ugly bastards. A hundred females and two males. The thing was, only one of the males could be 'beachmaster', getting to mate with each of the waiting women. They sorted it out though, throwing their heads back, hurling four gappy teeth at each other's throats – teeth powered by three tons of blubber. They bounced, thudded and tore at each other. I was transfixed by it, wouldn't let her turn it off. By the time the series ended she and I were pretty much an item.

She appreciated me all right. I'm a craftsman,

after all. It was a bit like tickling fish – holding her in suspense between her muscle spasms, flicking or not flicking that switch for her, as she waited, unbreathing, damp on the creased sheets. Every orgasm had her slipping more deeply onto me, wanting me more, becoming softer and more pliant. She became less siren, more spaniel. I don't always need to come, not every time. That kept me in control. I didn't want her trying to engulf me, making me feel I owed her.

The more pleasure I gave her, the more she wanted us to be together – holidays, that sort of thing. Maybe I wanted that too at one point. Or thought I did at the time. I liked the idea of sitting on a rocky shore up the west coast together. One of those places beginning with an A: Ardnamurchan or Acharacle or something. I've never been there, just seen pictures of sunshine and seals (the pretty dog-like ones; not the elephants). And we'd retreat to some country hotel where everyone would want to buy us drinks, thinking we were honeymooners, wanting to be close to us to regain a bit of something they'd had a taste of years back. We never did get around to it though.

All that togetherness stuff wasn't really me, anyway. You have to be careful, and don't I know it. I've done the 'hook, line and sinker' number. Fatal, if you let that happen with the wrong person. She always was the wrong person, despite the fun getting her in the first place, prising her away from that dickhead boyfriend of hers. I knew she wasn't for me in the long run – too clever, different class, all that sort of thing. I enjoyed my catch for a bit though.

I've had more women than fish suppers, I like it when they're a challenge. Tactics. 'Get them talking about their childhood, and you'll be sure of a shag.' That's what I always told the boys when they asked me how I did it. The fascination's been there since school. Even then I wanted to know women, their secrets, and I loved those biology lessons, learning about their parts and that. I told the

Careers Officer that I wanted to be a gynaecologist. What better way to get to know a whole heap of women? But you have to have exams for that. Mass shagging was easier. No exams necessary. (Though they tell me I'd pass one with flying colours if there was such a thing.) Anyway, it was probably the right choice. I've seen the way people talk to the dentist down the pub – the hand goes over the mouth; they go all tight-lipped. A gynaecologist might have a similar effect on women. That would completely defeat the purpose.

There were times when it felt so good with her, like we were really close. Sometimes she stroked my head and back as I drifted to sleep. I felt all my muscles easing out, flattening into softness under her hands. Felt like I was being spoilt for a wee while, like a big tomcat giving in to affection, purring. And there was the pineapple. She fed me pieces of it freshly sliced one morning while I was still half-asleep. 'You said you liked fresh fruit,' she said. The first bite squirted sweetness into my sandpaper morning mouth. She leant over me, ruffled with sleep and smiles, offering me juice soaked fingers to suck. It was almost too much for me. 'You can have me put down, now,' I said. 'I'll never get better than that.'

There was one night we were all tied up in the sheets, afterwards, as usual. Something welled up and came out as words. 'I want to be inside you,' I said. She giggled and slid on top of me again. But that wasn't really what I meant. I wanted to be under her skin, so close that I knew everything about her. I wanted to consume her, occupy her almost. It scared me, that outburst. What the hell was I on about? The words had jumped off my tongue without permission.

There were other scary times too. I used to wake in the night and look at her sleeping. She looked so wrapped up in herself, rather than in me. I felt a kind of tenderness, kissed her and called her 'my darling'. I thought I was going to cry, and I didn't know the reason. Believe me,

I know the fear when you wake up in a strange bed at six in the morning. I've scarpered out of many of those ones. This fear was different. It wasn't long after all that stuff we broke up. I remember kissing her eyes when the tears started to flow. It seemed a tender sort of gesture, but I also hoped the kisses would somehow block up the tears. But fuck it. I haven't thought about any of that for a long time, so why the hell am I digging it up now. Just because that face has appeared out of Planet Zog.

She's still looking down at me, shielded by the high side panels of the coach, still not acknowledging me. I feel stupid next to the package of nappies on the pavement, broadcasting whiffs of shit and milk if you get too close to me. Broadcasting the Friday nights that are a bit different these days – not down The Arches, but in front of the TV with a ready-prepared meal, taking it in turns to see to the wee boy. I always fight to be the one to go, right enough, to give him a squeeze and a song maybe. To make up for missing him during the day, thinking about his smile every five minutes.

Should I wave – what would she want? The engine's revving. The lights have turned green. Perhaps it's better to let it go; it's dead and buried. But if she was an old school pal, I'd have dragged her off the bus by now for a coffee. What's this daft pretence of not knowing each other. We could be friends now, couldn't we? I remember suggesting that when we split and she said, 'No thanks, I have enough friends.' That was pretty bitchy I thought.

Our gaze gets disconnected by the coach moving forward. Her chestnut hair swings over her shoulder as she turns to face the front. She reaches down, perhaps for her bag on the floor. I can almost sense that secret nobble at the top of her spine, the one I want to touch, to curl my body against. And I feel the after-burn of her gaze. It would be fun to catch that smile, and hear that giggle again. Then my hand is up, waving goodbye. But she doesn't even look back.

Life Drawing

I got the job without even taking my clothes off. It never occurred to me there'd be an interview. I imagined you'd get your kit off and give the whole staff a twirl, like a stage audition, them looking on with thumbs and forefingers on chins, clipboards even. And then they'd hold up score-cards, Eurovision-song-contest style.

I answered Trevor's questions.

– No, never done it before; there's a first time for everything!

– I guess it's just a job ... and I quite like a college atmosphere. Reminds me of being at school.

—Actually I've never tried keeping still for that long. But I'm very patient, and I think a lot – won't get bored.

– I don't think I know anyone here, no.

And the bearded eyes studied me, not undressing me, but trying to see my motivation for a difficult job with crap money.

I have my reasons. Perhaps it was the wording of the ad, the small word 'life' that attracted me when the paper fell open on the public library desk: 'Models wanted for life drawing. Male and female. Five pounds per hour.' And what I didn't tell Trevor; a job where I didn't need to speak. OK I'd be naked, there'd be people looking at me, but they wouldn't need to know me.

• • • • • • • • • • • • • • • • •

'It's the *pose* you're after,' says Trevor to his class, 'forget light and shade, look at the angle of the arms, the twists here. Amazing what the body can do.' And he points at a part of me as if I'm not in it. I become a machine and that suits me fine.

To start with the students exist to me as a semi-circular presence of boards, easels, and paint-splattered jeans. I can tell without looking at their faces that they frown and purse their lips. The room is heavy with concentration. Theirs and mine. You just hear the scratch of pencil or charcoal, the shuffle of feet as Trevor approaches and they make way for his superior eye, his chat.

'How's it going?'

'So-so … I'm having a bit of trouble with x, y or z.' / 'I think x has gone a bit y.'

'OK. Try using marks like these …' and he's away, re-shaping what they've done, imposing his view on their work. The students grunt, acquiesce, thank him.

And then it's the break and I un-rack myself. I go behind the screen to put on my robe – can't bear the intimacy of putting clothes *on* in public. Then the hard part – to drink coffee, co-exist as a human in the same room as the students. They're happy to ignore me; they gather around each other's work, chat, bang in and out through the swing-door for loos, coffee, whatever.

When they go out there's a chance to find out what they see when they look at me; how they interpret me. I vary. In some drawings I look too thin, in some too muscular, in others fatter than I would like. Mostly I have no face. There's angles, form, the suggestion of the pattern on the drape behind, but no face. They cannot read me. Thank God. Five minutes shrinks to seconds and we're called back by a clap of Trevor's hands. It's a relief to become a machine again.

•   •   •   •   •   •   •   •   •   •   •   •   •   •   •   •   •

The studio is quiet when I arrive each morning. Trevor's there, taking small gout-steps around the studio with his nose in a mug, the white beard collecting coffee droplets. His gut pushes against the fisherman's smock, the belly pockets bulging with pencils, paint-brushes, cigarettes.

'Ah, morning, super-model,' he says when he sees me.

I have no name.

There's a different pose each day. Today it's the couch. It might sound comfy but how would you like it? One buttock clinging to the edge of the couch and the other in fresh air supported by an outstretched leg, the upper body thrust back onto cushions, arms folded above my head. I try to wear a relaxed expression on my face. God knows why.

If I look downwards along my body in this pose, I can see the parting effect of gravity on my breasts, the rise of a not-so-flat belly and the knee and ankle of the curled leg. The ankle looks so far away, it hardly belongs to me. The dome of anklebone points at the ceiling. My strange ankle bones. 'Ankle and elbow joints like nipples,' he always said. He lies on his back on the old Indian rug we used to have, with my foot flat in the palm of his hand, as it dangles from my chair. Laughter throws him backwards. Regaining control, his head rises, the eyes return to the foot and its protruding ankle bone, and he shakes his head and smiles.

'Could you put your right foot back a bit?' A student's voice cuts into my thoughts. 'That's it.'

Sorry – that guy on the floor was distracting me. I wrote him a long letter actually. Six months after and I wasn't going to think of him anymore. I told him about my fresh start, told him he was a bastard for leaving me, but that I was going to be OK. I even put it in an envelope, then looked at it, wondering what to do with it. What was the address now? I left it inside my writing pad for a few days in the drawer, then I took it out and burned it. That was my real new start. There's a small cough nearby and I realize my head is levering backwards, pulled by the tightening neck muscles. I empty my head, relax.

As the days go on, I become more aware of the students, look at them obliquely when they don't realize. I look at their drawings too, but only when they leave the room. You pick it up. I heard some students in the cafeteria complaining about one of the other models, who visited them all during the coffee breaks, squatting down, still naked, 'dangling all his bits on the floor'. They don't want intrusion either.

I don't know their names. I only learned Nick's because of Trevor getting agitated with him.

'C'mon Nick, man, let's get the feeling for the form going. Fuck all the detail. Here, give me your pencil. B1? Use something softer for Christ's sake.' And after a few minutes I hear long lead lines being stroked onto Nick's paper. 'Get the feeling for the whole body.' Out of the corner of my eye, I see him hand back the pencil to Nick. Then he goes on to the next student.

Despite the tuft of goatee, Nick looks young. He's tall and gangly, one of the few students who work standing up, cocking his head to appraise his work with one leg crossed over the other. He reminds me of a cricket.

I make a particular point of looking at Nick's drawing when he leaves the room. From a distance you can tell where Trevor's pencil has been; length and fluidity. The hard long line of the outstretched leg, the other knee foreshortened, curled onto a different plane, the weight of the upper body pressed back. All expressed with a few simple lines. Yes, the pose *felt* like that. I have to move closer to see Nick's work. I see what Trevor means. The faint lines of detail confuse the eye against the sheer spaces of the naked form. The strangest thing is that my face has features worked into it. The eyes stare directly at the viewer; the face is in pain. The forehead puckers; the lips are full and sour. Why was he drawing it? This was defeating the point of the exercise. And though my eyes stare back at me now, I know damn well I never looked in his direction once.

There's a slight shuffle behind me and Nick looks down at me, smiling and pulling at his goatee, the other hand folded on the elbow.

'It's a good pose,' he says.

I pause before I answer, making him wait,

wanting to stay in control, give him access to less. 'Fancy swapping?'

And as he laughs, I move on to the next easel, pulling the robe tighter about me.

When I go back to the pose, I feel exposed.

•   •   •   •   •   •   •   •   •   •   •   •   •   •   •   •   •

The next day the studio welcomes me with the now familiar rush of turpentine and coffee up my nose. And a new pose. I'm to stand, holding the arms of a chair, leaning into it with my back to some of the class. Trevor says it'll be hard going, I can rest every half-hour. I release my hair from its clip so it curtains my face as I stretch forward. The semi-circle of eyes clamp me, start their analysis. I make myself machine again. The tilt of the upper body in space reminds me of diving. Just a little more forward motion and it would be a tumble towards the big studio window, with its release into a suburban cul-de-sac.

Windows. When the police came, they sat on the sofa, helmets in laps, and I sat on the moss-green velour armchair opposite. The armchair was arranged to give a view through the French windows onto the lawn. It was the first thing that came into my head when they told me; how am I going to mow the lawn? That was his job. The pull start has always been too difficult for me, too stiff.

Back at the studio window, a woman crosses the cul-de-sac with a shopping bag. She stalks down the hill. Even from here I can tell she's frowning, her body says it, with her coat whipping up around her legs in the wind.

My eyes drift to the car park immediately below. A man leans into the passenger seat of a grey car. I can only see his back, but I know it's him; the greying hair shaved up the back of the neck and the wide beige shirt that I gave him two birthdays ago tucked into straight jeans. Suede boots. He backs out of the car carrying a box and kicks the door shut. I'm ready to rush down the stairs, shake him by the shoulders, scream at him, 'But I thought you were dead. They told me you were dead.' But as he turns towards the building, I see that the buttons are wrong. On the shirt. Dark rather than pale. And the face is too thin; too old; too unkind. My body prickles in fury – tricked again.

'Need a break, super-model?' And although I'm aware that my arms are trembling and my neck in spasm, I think I'm still in the pose.

'No. I can hold it a bit longer.'

•   •   •   •   •   •   •   •   •   •   •   •   •   •   •   •   •   •

I pick out the dialogue between Trevor and Nick with relief.

'Better, Nick, better... much more feel for the overall form, a real sense of movement here. See if you can loosen it up even more. Try these sweeps here.'

During the break, I stretch my arms above my head, circle my head to free the shoulder muscles. I walk around the room to look at the drawings. The proportion of leg to arm has obviously been a problem. The drawings are mostly ugly and I resist the urge to laugh. Nick's drawing stops me. This time there's no face. The drawing is dynamic, more purposeful than the others. The lines are bold, smudged charcoal. He's captured something. The angle of the back and limbs, especially something about the head suggest a pull upwards. The drawing conveys the pull of shock; a transition out of composure; the spirit in a tangle with the body. I look around the room for Nick but he's not here. How did he dare? I leave the studio for the toilet.

•   •   •   •   •   •   •   •   •   •   •   •   •   •   •   •   •   •

By lunch-time I've recovered and am in the cafeteria dropping bits of cress out of a sandwich into the *Daily Mail*.

'Mind if I join you?' Nick plonks himself down opposite me, a plate of sausages and chips in front of him, all goatee and sloping shoulders. His hands are petite on the knife and fork. He sees me looking.

'Concentration makes me hungry – it's my main meal; don't eat much at night ...' He loads his fork and then his mouth with chips and ketchup, still chewing when he speaks. 'Trevor says life drawing's important because the naked body's the thing we all recognize most. We react to a live human presence.'

'Oh, really.' I ignore the question mark in his voice.

'Yeah, like it's something really fundamental we're looking for? "To be naked is to be oneself, without disguise," said ... ' he looks around for inspiration and then smiles, '... someone!'

'More mystical than a lump of middle-aged human flesh, then?'

'I just wondered how it felt for you, being the focus for all our learning, our ... discipline. All of us trying to get the greatest insight into human life by studying you.'

I look at him steadily; I have to stake out some fundamental ground here, but he carries on.

'I guess when I look at you with a pencil in my hand I'm looking for what's going on underneath.'

'It's a job. I earn five pounds an hour. And no one asks me difficult questions.'

Tomato ketchup slides off the fork in front of his mouth and drips onto the front of his check shirt. He wipes at it with a forefinger and sucks it.

'I guess it'll be a bit of extra for you – on top of your husband's salary?'

I nod, then catch my head. 'No!' Caught out by wanting to forget again. I don't really have to explain, do I? We fall silent for a moment.

'Your drawings ...' He looks up from his chips, perhaps happy to be drawn back to the subject. 'Well, maybe you should just be getting the mechanics right. You know, forget all this meaning of life stuff and, well, learn to draw?'

He doesn't respond. It's hard to tell if he even hears.

'What's your name anyway? I guess you're not really called "super-model"?'

• • • • • • • • • • • • • • • • • •

After lunch it's the same pose and there's no curtain of hair that can hide what my body seems to reveal. I am more naked than I've ever felt before. The scratch of each pencil illustrates my pain, outlines my anger. My hands grip the arms of the chair, force me through the minutes and hours to five o'clock.

I get dressed behind the screen. Slowly. I hear the studio empty, measured by the bang of the swing door with the rubber damper missing, the retreat of footsteps and voices up the corridor. I hear the studio fall quiet as the last one leaves.

His board on the easel is empty – he's taken the drawing down. But it doesn't take me long to find his portfolio, leaning against the wall behind where he works. I lay it flat on the floor, kneel down to undo the neatly tied ribbons and unfold the flaps. And there I am. I'm in date order, still acrid with the fixative spray they use to stop the charcoal smudging off. I lay each of the drawings flat on the floor and stand up to look at them. Two of them mock me, display my history to the spectator. Where could I end up? Perhaps framed at a posh exhibition or on the sitting room wall for his friends and family to admire.

I'm careful with the others – replacing them, still in date order, re-tying the bows. Then I pick up the one with the face. My fingernails shiver on the chalk-feel of the surface. The paper is tough and strong, resistant between my hands. The tear goes diagonally, separating upper and lower torso. But it's not enough; the face still stares back at me. I tear again and again until the pieces are so small they cease to offend. The second drawing is easy, my arms flex confidently until there's a frayed pile at my feet. My hands are black and some of it is probably smeared on my face. I feel triumph and relief.

The swing door bangs, and Trevor is there, looking at me. Then he's standing next to me, looking at the floor by my feet. Without turning, he cups a hand over the top of my shoulder.

'Are you OK, super-model?'

I feel the salt-heaviness rise at the back of my throat, and the novelty of tears on my face.

The Threshold

He needed a new cloth for the silver polish, one of those soft blue ones she kept under the kitchen sink. But there was no way he was going to leave the room. He made do with the blackened one, squirted polish onto it and picked up the first trophy, holding it for a moment double-handed above his head. Being a champion again tickled a smile onto his face. The trophy didn't need polishing that badly, but it was good to tackle them before they started to tarnish. It also gave him something constructive to do while he calmed his breath, sat out the trouble, and waited for the right moment to get out of the house. He rubbed the cloth over the looped letters of the title. 'Junior Boys Singles Champion'. Then he turned to the back of the cup for his name, three times among the winners: 1970 James Monty, 1971 James Monty, and 1972 James Monty. He'd been allowed to keep the trophy after he won it for the third time.

He sat on the pink counterpane in the sanctuary of the spare bedroom, the trophies next to him on a table. This was where he generally displayed them now, where they were best appreciated, where he could admire them while he worked out on his rowing machine. As he polished, the trophy rested against his bare legs, legs that were ready for action in white tennis shorts, tanned and licked with wiry fair hair.

Three bangs shook the door, each with a word attached.

'Get. Out. Here.'

Felicity's yowl jarred against his world, but he mentally picked up the intruder like a stray hair that spoils the surface of a smooth black suit, and cast it away. He lifted a corner of the counterpane to the trophy and buffed a brilliant final burnish onto it.

The door handle rattled.

'You dare lock the door on me.' Her words fell like darts into a cushion. There was a brief silence in which he picked up the next trophy, shook it high, double-handed, took a deep breath of pure air, and heard the roar of the crowd. Then, while he inspected the trophy for tarnish, more of her words crept in.

'Don't hide. We need to talk. You always hide.'

Felicity's lipstick smile had faded when they'd passed in the hall. He'd been heading for the tennis courts; she was coming in from her dance rehearsal. Or rather, they didn't pass; she didn't let him. She pushed him back into the flat a thump at a time. On his chest.

'Leave.

Her.

Alone.'

'She needs my help.'

'James, she does not. And nor does her teacher. Give them a break.'

'A break? That's just what I'm trying to do. Why shouldn't she get the chance?'

'Go and win the championship yourself if it's so important. But leave her out of it.'

Three strides and he would have been out the door. Running down the steps and over the road. But she'd winded him. So he turned back instead, into the spare room, for a different sort of victory.

•   •   •   •   •   •   •   •   •   •   •   •   •   •   •   •

He hadn't ever locked the door on her before. He often came into the spare room for a rowing workout and to polish the trophies. When he'd first started using the room, he'd left the door open, but it had gradually swung shut over the last year or so. It had felt good to lock the door. He'd felt the power rising in his body, the blood pumping to his head from his toes, as he'd overcome her in eye-to-eye combat across the threshold of the room. He clicked shut the last strip of her angry face and red dress, and then turned the key. It was like winning the final point of a tie-break. Total exhilaration.

But of course, since this victory, the adrenaline had started to drain and he'd climbed off his podium. As he distracted himself with the trophies, he craved a cigarette. He clamped his teeth down on the white plastic dummy she'd bought him, the mock cigarette to get him off the real thing, and twirled it in his mouth like a Clint Eastwood cheroot. He had a suspicion she'd got it to make him look stupid, to punish him for his 'habit'. He crossed the room to the window and squashed his left cheek against the glass, as he often did, so he could glimpse the tennis courts across the rec. He could pick out Mandy's pink Lycra shorts, amongst the junior group who were being coached, but he couldn't really see how she was playing.

A tearing sound outside the locked door pulled his head away from the window. The sound leaked into the room through the cracks between frame and door. It came at regular intervals, like the dripping of a tap. Sharp and unsettling.

Then the smell took the same route into the room.

It was familiar but he couldn't quite place it. It wasn't cigarette smoke. Nor cigars. It was the sort of smoke that made him cough, just as he did now, when she first started to light the fire in the front room. It jabbed at him, acrid and sharp. It was usually short-lived, soon overtaken by the more mellow aroma of smoke from twigs and logs.

He stood in the middle of the room and stared as smoke trickled under the door, and formed a dark column up the white paintwork. He nodded. She was burning newspaper outside the door. Trying to smoke him out. He knew very well where she'd got the idea from. Felicity always laughed when she told how her mother used to threaten to smoke her father out of his study when he didn't appear promptly at meal times. It had sounded like a family joke, not something that anyone would do.

'What the fuck are you doing?' A cough tore into his throat, bent him double.

There was no answer, but he could hear the steady tear of paper. She'd be ripping pages of the *Daily Mail* into narrow strips, working from edge to edge, slowly splitting the grins of Mel C or Tony Blair and amputating sportsmen's legs. He'd watched her do it in the front room many times, pausing when she found showbiz gossip to read out to him, or pictures of ballroom dancers which were too precious to shred.

'You're a mad bitch, Felicity.' He wondered how she could be so careless of their paintwork and carpets – they'd only finished decorating a few weeks ago. She'd been so proud of it.

He crossed the room to open the windows. But as he tried each catch in turn, in accelerating rattles, he realized they were all locked. He had no idea where the keys were, and lapped the room, buckling forward to cough, and stretching up to shelves and ledges where keys might be hidden. He pitched around the room, like a deranged animal confined by walls. He'd seen zoo keepers on TV dropping nets over them and knew that they struggled themselves into an even worse snare. It was better to be still. He sat back down on the bed, took up a trophy and the cloth, found his name and began to rub. But the coughs broke his concentration, and his eyes ran too much to see whether he was making a good job of it.

He bundled the pink counterpane off the bed and stuffed it against the door. It reminded him of being a kid. He and his brother Ian used to block out the sound of their parents fighting downstairs. They'd locked out the noise with blankets stacked against the door; it kept them safe while they carried on playing. That was before their father had left, taking Ian with him.

He tried to slow his breathing. The door handle rattled.

'Go ahead, burn the house down.' He coughed the words into a handkerchief.

She said something but he couldn't hear it clearly now. It was muffled by the counterpane. He just caught the words 'talk' and 'try'.

The rattling stopped. He put his ear to the door. There was no sound of tearing now but he heard a rustle of clothing as she moved on the other side of the door. It summoned a ludicrous image. She was stamping, screaming and kindling bonfires, still in the red ball gown she'd been wearing for her rehearsal with Roddy, her dicky-bowed partner.

James couldn't understand her new passion for ballroom dancing. She was already entering competitions. It seemed to him a bizarre way to spend time. The lengthy preparations sickened him – fixing her smiles on with lipstick, applying mascara, and sequins. It was like putting on a coat of varnish. 'I danced at school,' she'd said. 'And anyway I might as well do something fun. You're obviously not going to give up your sports to do things with me.' He'd gone along to watch once, because Mandy wanted to go. He'd seen the way Roddy smiled at Felicity and put his hand on her back in the tight fitting dress. When he watched them wiggle through the Samba, he'd had to look away. He'd argued with her afterwards. He told her it had made him feel sick, that Roddy was such a slime-ball. James slept under the pink counterpane in the spare room that night.

And now she was parading her torturer's costume. She was homing right in on his weakness. She knew about his lungs. She wanted him to suffocate. He'd seen her devious strategies, the ones that won her Monopoly and produced her tight-mouthed winner's smiles. But this was a dangerous determination he'd not seen before.

An electric whirr now started outside the door. Was she drying her hair? Smoke gushed, air-assisted past the folds of the counterpane into the room. It rose to deepen the storm cloud clinging to the bedroom ceiling. He had no idea how to escape it.

An electronic screeching pierced his head like needle and thread, ear to ear. The smoke alarm.

He felt like he'd smoked eighty fags. He was clogged with smoke. He covered his nose and mouth, tied a towel around his ears. The smoke was thick, the whine stung him. It was a kind of hell. Smoke, screeching, and a demented wife dancing across his path. He pulled a chair over so he could reach the smoke alarm, and took the battery out.

He rattled again at a window catch, and pressed his cheek to the glass. Mandy was there in the pink shorts, in a row of children at one end of the court. On the other side of the net a row of children fed balls to them. They were practising backhands. She missed one, hit one into the net, hit one ballooning high into the back fence of the court. 'Come on Mandy,' he said to himself. 'You're playing crap.' If only he could have been there, she wouldn't be playing like that. He held an imaginary racquet, turned his shoulders and hips to strike a topspin backhand. 'That's how to do it.' She just needed him to polish up her style.

Then she hit a whopper, sliced hard and flat just over the net. He leapt upwards, arms above his head cupping the trophy that would be hers.

Mandy's coach, the Fat Cow appeared. At first, he'd heard the mutterings of other parents about him through Felicity. Not long after, the Fat Cow had written a letter asking that, 'Mr Monty stay away from the coaching sessions'. She complained that he had been disruptive and was 'too competitive on his daughter's behalf, considering this is a class for eight- to ten-year-olds of mixed ability.'

'Rubbish. At least I get some decent strokes out of her,' he told Felicity. 'The Fat Cow just doesn't like the competition from me – you know, maybe I'm a better coach.'

This was one of the times when the waste of his own talent had risen up to choke him.

'Look at me,' he'd said. 'Look what happened to my sports when Dad wasn't around to push me.'

'I've heard it before,' said Felicity. She stood with her back to him, her rubber-gloved hands paddling at the washing up.

His career had foundered when he missed getting into the Boys Fourteen-and-Under Team because his mother couldn't afford the extra coaching. That was the end really. As a consolation, she'd taken him on a holiday to his grandmother's in Devon. He'd spent two weeks swimming up and down in an angry line parallel with the beach.

Now he had a humdrum job as a sports teacher. Twice a week in the summer he gulped down post-match tea and cakes after playing local league tennis.

'Even the spotty kids at school have heard of Dad and Ian. They're household names,' he complained to Felicity. 'But *James* Monty. Nobody's ever heard of *James*.' He wondered how things might have turned out if he'd stayed with his father instead of Ian, and if God's gift to football himself had stayed with their mother. There would have been no expensive training and celebrity lifestyle for Ian then. His father had died a few years before in a hotel blaze in Mallorca and the funeral had brought him and Ian together for the first time in many years. A concealed boil of bitterness in James had burst through to the skin.

'At least you had a father, you had a chance,' he'd said to Ian, whose head was weighed down with tears. 'All I had was a gap. A tennis racquet without the strings.'

Felicity belittled his concerns about the past. Last week she'd knelt in front of his armchair in the front room and said, 'James, grow up. You really can't take it out on us anymore. You must forget it.' And she'd started her crying thing when he got up to go to the rowing machine.

Now he was watching his daughter, the future star, through a haze of smoke, choked back from helping her succeed.

'How's it in there now?'

He didn't answer.

'I'll bloody well get you out here to talk about it.'

'I'd rather die.'

'Bastard. Stubborn bastard.'

Her voice was sounding unhinged now, a screech decorating the first syllable. It pleased him. He heard the thud of her palms on the door, a whimper. Her frustration warmed him. She knew she wasn't winning.

Then it went quiet, and he heard thuds from their bedroom next door. He couldn't imagine what she was doing. It occurred to him that he could sneak out now. But the thought of being caught by her, tiptoeing across the hall carpet, stopped him. Her body would be twitching with rage, she'd still be wanting to talk. Her and her tittle tattle. Couldn't she get all the talk she needed these days from Roddy and the ballroom? Talking wasn't ever going to help Mandy succeed.

Bang. Low down on the door, as if it had been kicked. Then there was a more distant thud, like the front door banging. He went back to the window and saw her out in the street, slamming the boot of the car. He wondered what she had put in it. He watched her kangaroo-hop the car to the tennis court entrance, where she jumped out again. She'd changed out of her sequins and into her beige trouser suit. It was an outfit he rather liked. She walked right onto the court, and took Mandy by the hand. The cough grabbed him, juddered his eyeballs. When his sight cleared again Felicity and Mandy were hand in hand, speaking to the Fat Cow. The racquet he had bought her for Christmas trailed from Mandy's hand, its head resting on the court. As they turned, Felicity cast one look towards the house. Her auburn hair prickled around her face and he could imagine the stubborn set of her mouth. They were in the car, heads bent, fiddling with straps, and then quickly out of sight down the road.

So Mandy was missing her lesson completely now. Brilliant. She'd fail just like he did. James gathered up all his ambitions for her in a fist. He thrashed it in an overhead smash against the window, clean through the glass, bursting the vapour barrier so that as the smoke seeped out, the Fat Cow's fog of platitudes trickled in.

'Good girl.'

'Nice shot, Chloe.'

'Lovely!'

He'd broken out of the cage, shattered his sanctuary. He barely registered the neighbour digging her front garden who stopped and looked up at the window

He became aware of the dripping at about the same time as the pain in his hand. He cradled it, watching the drips quiver off his hand with each cough. They tapped onto the cream carpet. It had been a ridiculous colour to choose, he'd told her that all along. He just watched, glad of the damage as the blood spots soaked deep into the fibres.

A noise outside summoned his gaze. He looked through the jagged hole in the window, straight across to the rec. The splatter of blobs were starting to bleed down the glass. Some scruffy boys, probably his own pupils, were kicking a football around. The sound didn't belong to them. A dog snaked across the grass, its nose pulled along on a track of scent. Noiseless. A child in a red coat stood on the grass, straight-legged and staring upwards. Above her, a matching red balloon soared. She wailed after the vanishing string.

He went back to the bed and started polishing again. 'Most Promising Junior,' James Monty 1972. But his hand hurt too much to lift it this time and he printed fingerprints of blood onto the silver. They spoilt the brightness.

There was nothing to stop him now. He was free.

He turned the key and stepped into the hall, where he breathed smokeless air, and stood with one tennis shoe in the metal pan of ashes Felicity had left.

Ever Onward to Victory

I never visited this city when I was alive, nor the country, though of course I knew it was famous for whisky and socialism. I used to read Robert Louis Stevenson to the men in the Sierra Maestra, between fighting engagements, to take their minds off fear. But I didn't know much more than that. And now, however much I might want to debate their future over shared food and drink, and salute their anti-imperialist struggle, I can only observe, limping on the outermost periphery of mortality with my one remaining sense.

    I peer down. A troop of young men parade along a narrow street of pubs and after-hours shops, their heads pushed back by the upturned bottles at their lips. I linger a little to understand better. What will revolutionary men do here? They break into a run, tossing the bottles between them. Action. That first flutter of action. Will they do more? Come on, my friends, more. A bottle flies into a shop window, sending a stack of glass shivering like fish scales to the floor. I have to twist the arm of my imagination to remember how it would sound. Would it be like the burst of a grenade against tin – one of those explosions when it's the splinters of silence afterwards that shatters onlookers the most? The young men dance some slick, rehearsed steps – reaching into the shop window through a jagged hole. One man passes the items into waiting arms. As each one is loaded up, he runs away down the street with his hoard. They dissolve from each other into the night.

    A strange figure shuffles in behind them. Her lips move, apparently in speech, but she's alone, not part of the dance of the young men. She plunges head and shoulders through the jagged hole. Her arms flap inside like a swimmer, and then she backs out, her coat protecting her from the sharp spars. A couple of large tartan blankets and a jumper follow her out of the hole, and she returns for two small glass bottles of something brown – whisky I guess.

She stuffs them down the front of her overcoat and glances in each direction. I move in closer to her, match her gaze through the glass towards what's left of the window display. I share her dilemma, as the time to grab dwindles and the risk of being caught swells. What would I take if I was her? Little is left. No food or weapons.

Then a small red tin locks my gaze. I know why. I'd have chosen that tin for my ammunition had I been alive. I'd love to feel its weight in my hand, full of bullets. The reassuring rattle. It would become a friend I couldn't be without.

She doesn't reach for it. She turns away. I want to push her back, to make her live for me. I'm jealous of the chance to breathe vitality into tomorrow – to roll out of bed in the morning to fight for something. To need to win. She's not going to do it for me. My arm gets greedy to be flesh again, to disobey the rules. I reach forward for the tin myself.

Cold. I have sensation. Finger tips on cold metal. Slippery. My fingers curl under the smooth surface, lift the tin from the cloth beneath it. The weight rests on the palm of my hand. I'm back in the living world. Life strikes all my missing senses, seizing me for a second like an electric shock. A fog of sweated cider from the woman by my side hits the back of my throat, closing it down to air. It reminds me of the asthma I used to suffer.

The woman waddles a few steps then turns and looks straight at me.

'Is that all you're taking?' she says. 'C'mon son, we'd better be away. They'll be here any minute.'

She speaks straight to me. Compassion from a live being almost whips up tears. I run after the scuffling figure, laughing as soft petals of rain flutter on my face. She's given me an earthly status. It reminds me of my travelling days – the joy of encounters with people like her. How real the world felt then.

•　•　•　•　•　•　•　•　•　•　•　•　•　•　•　•

We sit side-by-side in a doorway at the top of a set of steep, dark steps. This is a good start to surviving on the road again. I relish the cold soaking upwards from the concrete under my backside. The smell of urine. This is the familiar paradox of the guerrilla fighter – morale soaring in proportion to discomfort. We swig the whisky. It spreads hot coals through my nose, throat, belly.

The woman's feet are stretched out in front of her, she has shoes that are worn and scuffed. She rolls down a thick wool sock that seems to be stuck to her ankle with a glue of dirt. A syringe sits against her skin.

'That's where I keep it,' she says.

I nod.

'Sometimes I inject the others. In the toilets.'

This reminds me of Alberto, when we travelled together, injecting me with adrenaline for my asthma attacks. You need friends like this when you're falling on the mercy of the byways.

'I was a doctor too,' I say. 'But I gave it up to fight.'

She falls asleep not long after that, propped against the door, her booty clutched to her front. I take the chance to cherish mine.

The tin is smooth and cool. I glide a finger across the lid and it bumps over a raised ribbon effect in one corner. There's a picture. A group of men in front of mountains and sea. They all wear kilts. They look like they have been living in the jungle, in the hills, for many days. They are warriors with big blades and swords. They wear berets a little like mine (I put my hand to my head and am reassured by the scratch of coarse cloth. It is still there). A man is stepping onto a boat, tall above his friends in the centre of the picture. You can see that the others adore and admire him. They seem to protect him, their eyes casting in different directions, alert to enemies, but allowing him as a centre of stillness among them. Perhaps he is the one who leads the common people to victory.

I know the faces on the tin; the faces of the

soldiers. I saw them myself in the Sierra Maestra. There's a photo I used to carry in my pocket. Yes – it's still here. Soft battered paper; black and white. A group of rebel soldiers, some sitting, some standing, so close that their clothes graze each other. All bearded. They face the camera, so there's no eye contact between them. They are the stillness in the midst of battle, in the midst of fear, post-coital after killing. They don't speak. Their eyes seek outwards in different directions. Their bodies are still, their minds furtive in the jungle, searching for crackles of concealment, flickerings of betrayal. I was one of them.

The photo. The tin. Even without turning over for the printed explanation, I see that these are noble men, who knew they were nothing; nothing in isolation from each other. They were brave fighters just as we were, perhaps more so. They fought with blades rather than guns, getting close enough to smell the ripe fear of their enemy. They rammed metal into another body, penetrating their enemy's darkness; unfolding their own.

I lift the lid and find something wrapped in clear plastic. It's a circular disc of biscuit which crumbles into fan shapes in my hands. I taste a corner. Sugar and salt. It sticks to my teeth, coats my tongue in a floury rich sweetness. This is soldier's food. Compact and full of calories, for proud men with the future in their faces. How wonderful that this struggle of the past, and of today, is celebrated in containers for food – for anyone and everyone to understand their place in history. Sugar and good fortune course through my veins.

My friend snores on next to me. But my senses are quivering too much with newly rediscovered sensation to stay put for long. I walk the streets.

•   •   •   •   •   •   •   •   •   •   •   •   •   •   •   •   •

'Cuba Libre' the sign says, and through the window I see bottles and glasses and teeth flashing in exchanges of laughter. I have to go in. I slouch at the bar with the one beer I can afford to buy. I look around to find out why it has the name. A few black and white photos are on the wall, showing Havana tenements and 'Club Tropicana' girls. There's a map of Cuba behind the bar, cut out of a plank of wood. Santa Clara isn't on it. Not even marked. I swivel my gaze to take in the Friday night youngsters, clean and groomed among the chrome shiny furniture. You can't tell by looking at them that salsa is playing. Their bodies don't connect. You would think it's only me that hears it. It's only me that's transported back across my life, across the world, with my hand flat on the back of a girl who moves sleek against me.

I down the last inch of my beer and feel in the pocket of my combat trousers. I already know the answer. There's nothing there. But I'm not leaving, not yet. I look around for a target. Along the bar there's a man in a yellow T-shirt. He looks bored, sipping at some sort of cocktail with a paper umbrella prodding him in the eye. I sigh deeply and utter a few words to my beer glass, remonstrating at it with my hands. It's an intimate dialogue. The yellow man notices, I know he does by the way he twitches his head a little and shifts his weight on the stool. I look up and smile.

'Daiquiri?' I ask.

He looks blankly at me. For a moment I fear I'm not visible for him, but then I see the change in his face colour, and he says, 'I'm sorry. I don't speak Spanish.'

'Daiquiri – your drink. From Cuba, no?' I exaggerate my accent.

His face lights up with understanding. 'So that's how you pronounce it.'

We laugh together and I slap my hand on the bar to show him how much I enjoy the joke.

'Where are you from?'

'Ah my friend, many places, many times. Argentina originally, though I spent several years in Cuba,'

I gesture at our surroundings as if we are, in fact, in Cuba.

I see his face go blank as he checks through associations and he says, 'Argentina? Didn't we have a war?'

'Nothing to do with me,' I laugh. 'That was years after I left.' I leave a pause and then slap the side of my face. 'Friend – what date is this?' It didn't matter what he said.

'1st June.'

'How could I forget?' I shake my head. 'My friend, this is the anniversary of the day I left my country. The last time I saw my mother, my family.'

'Really?'

'So sad that I cannot celebrate.' I allow a slump over my empty glass. 'I was robbed you see, when I arrived in this city. All my money gone.'

He jumps up and thrusts a hand into his jeans pocket. 'Here, I'll get you a beer.'

I protest a little. Only a little. When I finish the beer, he tries to get me another.

'No my friend. It's not right, drinking like this. In my country it is our custom to eat when we drink.'

And before long I have another beer and a large bowl of *patatas fritas* that spread a sheen of grease onto my fingers and lips. The man seems happy too. Happy to redistribute his wealth. Even if it is to a ghost. When he leaves, he slaps me on the back like I'm a long-lost friend and says something about Las Malvinas and no hard feelings. I'm left with an inch of beer, a warmth in my belly, and a reluctance to leave.

• • • • • • • • • • • • • • • • • •

Walking away down the cobbled street a couple pass me with a man propped up between them. He's singing. When he sees me, his head swings around in a double take and he raises a drunken fist in salute. I salute him back. Recognition.

'Where's the party, pal?' he shouts over his shoulder after me. 'I'll come as Mao Tse-Tung.' He folds forward, breathless with laughter. As they slide off into the night I hear him say, 'Had him on my wall when I was a student.'

Now I need to sleep. I would rather die than accept the bourgeois comfort of a hostel. This was a principle when I travelled and I'm not going to change it now just because I'm dead. And so I crawl into the back of a parked lorry for the night.

•   •   •   •   •   •   •   •   •   •   •   •   •   •   •   •   •   •

When I scramble out in the morning to get my bearings in the daylight, I think for a minute I'm in Chile. It's like the open-cast copper mine I visited with Alberto in the barren heart of the Altacama desert. Very like Chuquicamata. It is a village of work, men scrambling over a mountain like demented insects. The scene vibrates with mechanical thuds. And it's backed by a grey escarpment just like at Chiquicamata where the mountain was cut into enormous terraces to allow extraction. When I look more carefully, I see that the mountain here is made up of bricks and twisted steel cable, cast away gates and girders. And the escarpment is an ancient rock face, not man-made. I know that I am in 1999, in Edinburgh rather than Chile, by the look of the men with their white, white skin, the buzz of vehicles with orange flashing lights, the high necks of the cranes overseeing activity. And here maybe they're not watched over by bosses in large cars who mock them with inadequate wages. Maybe here where they have overthrown imperialism, it is different.

A queue of men twist towards a caravan, their boots coated in mud, their hands dangling mallets, crowbars, hammers. They leave the caravan and sit on the edge of the pavement, holding plastic cups to their lips. They are still and quiet, puffing at cigarettes, glancing at newspapers. They don't look at each other. I join them with a cup of coffee, extending the row on the pavement edge, providing a contrast in my combat gear, to their workers' uniforms – helmets, fluorescent jackets, loose boots and jeans. They continue to look at papers, chomp on rolls, grunt the odd remark. They have the stillness of men at rest, men who know the next few hours are going to be earnest toil. Their tools rest in the road.

'What is it you're building here?' I ask.

One or two of them look up, the bearded one at the end of the row leans forwards so he can see my face.

'Christ, where you been the last year mate?' The others laugh. I shrug. I've never been ashamed to ask questions.

'It's Donald's house,' a small man with a stripe of black on one cheek says.

'And who is this Donald?'

More laughter. 'Our new prime minister or whatever you call it.'

'And he needs a house?'

'Fuck's sake.' The striped man raises his eyes skyward. 'It's the parliament. For the big men to hang out in and decide our future.' He cranes backwards to contemplate the mountain of rubble for a moment and then points at the top of it with his folded newspaper. 'You can just see 'em, eh? Ruling from a pile of shit …' he turns and points his newspaper towards the rest of the city, the country, whatever, '… over a pile of shit.' He opens his newspaper and sinks his head back into its pages.

A lorry passes, sprinkling dust and diesel fumes into our cups of coffee. The men don't seem to notice but I feel my chest tighten with the first spasm of a cough.

'And so, you are building your own democracy? You must be proud of your work, no?' The row of heads remain pulled downwards by newspapers, coffee cups, other priorities, until the man at the end pipes up.

'I tell you, I'm proud when I get down the pub

with my pay packet on a Friday night. After a few pints.' He pulls at his beard. 'That's when I feel proud.'

'It says in the paper this place is going to cost a hundred and nine million,' says the striped man. 'Christ's sake. They could give every bugger in the nation a few pints for that. That'd be democracy, eh? That'd give us all something to smile about.'

I feel in my bag and bring out the biscuit tin, staring for a moment at the brave faces of the men in kilts; the one with the beard who regards his leader with fond eyes. I look over it to the men in front of me. I take off the lid and pass the tin down the line. The bearded man spits onto the road next to him.

'Here, cat.' I say.

'Cheers,' they mutter as they snap fist-sized portions from the petticoat tails. The bottom part of the tin is returned to me with a tiny corner of biscuit remaining. I hold the lid up to them.

'This man.' I point to the standing man, the one the others seem to respect and adore. 'Do you know him?'

Two of them screw up their eyes at it.

'Teuchters,' one of them mutters.

The bearded one reaches along the line to grab it from my hand and presses a finger ingrained with mud onto the chest of the loved man. 'Ah, the young pretender.' He throws the lid back to me. 'Poofta.'

'Sorry – "Poofta"?' I use my shirt to wipe dust from the lid after its fall into the road.

'Aye, dressed up in a female's clothes and that. Poofta.' He waits for me to show a sign of understanding but I shake my head.

'Ho-mo-sex-u-al,' He stabs each syllable at me with his rolled up newspaper. '*Comprendez*?'

'You don't honour him now? He did something for you, for the country?'

'Who are you anyway – a bloody journalist or something?'

I look at the man in the picture on the tin. 'I was like this man I think.'

They all look at me now, a row of eyes fanning out above the pavement edge.

'Time's up,' one of them says.

'Here,' I rummage in my pocket. 'I have a photo I can show you.'

They are standing up, picking up their tools, and shuffling in their big boots back towards the mountain. They mutter, pass stifled laughs between them. I stand up. Why should I be humble just because I have come without invitation into this place, into today's world?

'I paid in blood – to defeat imperialism. To free exploited workers. I inspired hatred of the enemy.' I bang the back of my hand against the photograph. 'I made these men into soldiers of freedom.' But the workers turn their backs on me, like turtles protecting their soft undersides.

'C'mon, boys,' one of them says, pointing his crowbar at the others like a gun, 'Back to the war-zone until the lunch break.'

I sit on my own and chew on the last piece of shortbread, coughing painfully on crumbs and anger, emptying the tin. Another group of workers arrives at the caravan. Taking what they are given. Not a speck of fight in one of them.

As I walk away from the building site, I pause. The empty tin is light in my hand. Yesterday, it was my trophy, accompanying the treasure of a new-found place on earth. Now it hardly seems worth keeping, with the shortbread gone. An empty receptacle. I have no bullets to keep in it so what use can it be?

I toss it high over a fence onto the mountain, to become part of the pile of shit. I watch it arch upwards, spinning against a grey sky and wait for the clatter. But when it lands I hear nothing. My vision closes in. There are black edges. I look at life through a porthole.

Then I'm on my back and I know I'm losing my

grip on the living world again. Being robbed of my full senses. My head rolls to one side. My remaining sense presents the neat cobbles and lawns of an ancient building – I read the sign: The Palace of Holyroodhouse. Does that mean Kings and Queens? I twist my head the other way and see the parliament mountain. The parliament that is a pile of shit. These institutions face to face? The laugh takes my penultimate living gasp. I expend the last one on the whisper '*Hasta la victoria siempre*' – ever onwards to victory. I excavate this reflex from deep in my veins. It disguises disappointment. And then I'm retreating to the sidelines, giving up my place on earth, observing the scene through a now comforting haze. Victory here is kept tightly packed in stories and shortbread tins. Tomorrow I'll look for other struggles.

Holiday Money

When he squatted next to me on the beach, the first thing I noticed was his arm. The curve of biceps began just above the elbow and led inside the sleeve of his Hard Rock Café t-shirt.

'Hi Lady. You like cigars?'

'No thanks. I don't smoke.'

'Maybe your husband?' He searched the immediate area with his eyes.

'No husband.' Dead.

'You take some for a gift, for a friend. Special from Cuba.'

'I don't think so.'

'Very good price. In the shops eighty dollars. I give you for twenty-five dollars.'

Ah, handling stolen goods then. Forget it, my boy. He brought out of his shoulder bag a wooden box decorated with two figures touching fingers over a balcony. He placed the box just above my knees as my legs stretched out on the sun-lounger. I was suddenly conscious of my middle-aged flesh rolled out like uncooked pastry in front of this boy in his, what – early twenties?

'See, *amiga*. Romeo and Juliet.'

'Very nice.' But no.

He leant towards me, unfastened the clasp at the front of the box and raised the lid, releasing an aroma of something like horseshit. Rows of cigars like brown sausages were tucked into neat lines inside. He pulled one out and put it into my hand. It felt dry and flaky. Hours of Cuban sun had been rolled into it. He had a good marketing technique. They did here. From where I was sitting, I could hear the sales pitch of the cocktail barman, singing, 'Daiquiri, piña colada, Cuba libre,' from under his thatch on the beach. He coupled the rhythm of Tito Puente with the grit of a London newspaper seller.

'Very nice.' I closed the lid and handed the box back to him. We smiled at each other. I hoped he had accepted my refusal, but he wasn't moving on to the next sun-spread tourist. I noticed he had slumped back from the squat into the sand so that he was now sitting next to me, his shoulder bag between his feet. We both looked towards the sea.

In front of us a man had beached himself, his belly doming high towards the sun. It was shiny with sun oil. The pharmaceutical coconut smell was cloying even from here. His arms were spread wide, his head low and unsupported on the sand. The extremities of his arms and legs flapped slightly. I hoped he wasn't stuck. I didn't feel like effecting a rescue.

'German?'

'No, English.'

'Ah, English. Is a good country, no? You like Cuba?'

'Love it.'

'You like to see some famous places?' He turned his gaze inland. A pile-carpet of forest was rolled out over sharp mountains. The buildings of the town aspired up to them. 'Churches, sugar mills. Very old. I take you. I know very well.'

'I don't think so. Thank you.'

'In town, there's very nice restaurant my friend runs. In his house. Very good food. You like fish?'

'Yes. But I get all my meals here.' I waved my hand behind my head at the ship-like hotel grounded on the beach behind me.

'Lady.' He reached forward and fingered the immovable plastic wristband clamped on me by the hotel when I arrived. 'This doesn't mean you must stay here. You're no slave to this place.'

His thumb and finger dented my wrist. And as our hands were side by side, there lay the contrast between the colour of his skin and mine. My eyes skipped up to his. How could I help being flattered by his attention? And then

Carol seemed to appear at my elbow, in her sensible shoes and business suit saying 'Mother, what exactly do you think you're doing?'

•   •   •   •   •   •   •   •   •   •   •   •   •   •   •   •   •   •

The heat and humidity squeezed me even more in the town. I took a break from exploring the patios, plazas, and towers and headed for the smoked glass air-con cool of the dollar shop. I grabbed a bottle of *agua mineral* and joined the queue of dollar-rich Cubans which trailed along the glass case towards the till. The cool brought back my brain a little. I cast my eye over what the fortunate could buy. Rose-scented soap, lipstick, matches, cigarette lighters, jelly, biscuits, and towards the back of the shop, microwaves, fridges and electric fans with big price tags. A man left the shop and walked away down the street with a toilet bowl on his shoulder competing in height with his straw hat.

The queue shuffled forwards as each conversation at the till came to a natural close. As I waited, delighted to be slow in the cool, the sound of hooves on cobbles took my attention through the glass shop front onto the street. I still hadn't got used to the novelty of the neat ponies who carried men in broad-brimmed hats and spurs through the streets. The view of the pony was obscured by half-a-dozen people clustered around the door, faces contorted in the effort to view the shelves. One of them, nose and forehead squashed to the glass, hands splayed above his head to blacken his reflection, looked familiar. He was wearing a Hard Rock Café t-shirt. It was the boy from the beach.

As I came out onto the pavement, the heavy dampness of the air, the smells of food cooking and rotting fruit wrapped themselves around me, strait-jacketed me. I had only been in the air-con a few minutes but had already become unaccustomed to the street.

'Hey, lady! Remember me?' His long limbs

bounded towards me along the pavement. He was taller than I'd realized before, his face shaded by a baseball cap.

'Yes. From the beach.' We shook hands. It was almost like meeting a friend in the street at home. And it was good to have a reason to stand still for a moment.

'You buy water only?' He put his hands to his shaking head. 'Lady, you could buy, anything ... the world!'

I looked back into the shop. Rose-scented soap was not the pinnacle of my dreams. 'Yes, but I can go shopping at home.'

'Of course. Is easy for you.' He looked back through the shop window for a moment. 'You can buy bluejeans in your country?' He slapped his thighs as he said 'bluejeans'. His smile radiated enthusiasm. I felt myself reflecting it back at him.

'Yes.'

'Ah. Levi's – they the best, no?'

'So my children tell me.' And he nodded, a look of longing on his face as he pondered the slimfit status they would give him.

'Let's go. I show you the town.' It was a change to have a companion to walk with. But Carol came along too. Stalking along just behind us. Frowning.

• • • • • • • • • • • • • • • • • • •

Later that afternoon I wrote postcards by the swimming pool, sitting well back from the edge to avoid the tidal waves as twenty or so German women surged and wobbled through an aqua aerobics session. 'Today I had a guide to the town,' I wrote, 'A young man.' Bound to get a reaction with Karen and Louise. The dreadful duo. They flashed in front of me, arms folded, smiling and nodding 'I told you so' at me. 'See what a bit of Cuban rum and holiday spirit can do for your love life, girl.' It was all very well for them, they were a good bit younger than me. But the fantasy invaded my body. It took root and grew as the afternoon heat thumbed my eyelids down. It was not unwelcome.

It's night. But there's some soft light, from a candle perhaps. And the room opens onto a veranda or a balcony through which wafts the palm tree rustle, the croak of harmless insects and jasmine scent. My shoulders are bare and have a soft (young) sheen in this light. And his t-shirt fabric clings and slips over the slope of his chest. We're relaxed. Drinking something. Opposite each other at a table. My body acts for me without preparation. I put my hand on his and continue to talk, as with one of my fingers I trace the long muscle from wrist to elbow, turn at the elbow and continue under the edge of the t-shirt sleeve over the taut skin on his upper arm. The skin is black satin, woven oil. I span the strength of revolutionaries with my hand. And somewhere in between then and the bit where we're in bed, the clothes come off. Invisibly. With the noise of silk static. And his voice in my ear is mango, sliced with a silver knife. There's cloves and coffee on his breath. When I kiss the dip in his chest, there's sea salt and spray. The night is like chocolate liqueur dripped drop-by-drop onto my tongue.

And as my eyes refocused on the glare of white-backed postcards slipping sweaty across my lap, there was a thunderous rumble of rocks as my mother turned in her grave.

• • • • • • • • • • • • • • • • • •

'You have to go to the Valle de los Ingenios. Is very interesting. Very old. Many tourists like.' He was in the hotel lobby, waiting for me two days later.

'What's *ingenios*?'

'The place where they made sugar. The rich people. Let's go. I take you.' Not long afterwards, I was in the back of some fifties American car driven by a friend of his. The windows in the front were open and he rested his elbow high on the door top and flashed smiles back at me.

I sat low in the back. Despite the rips in the leather seats out of which grey stuffing escaped, I felt the breeze catch my hair, remembered some ancient sensation. Could it be of glamour? Probably not. Carol would say that was ridiculous. I was in a dangerous situation.

The rear end of the car seemed to sink and trail as we graunched out of town. We swerved to avoid the cyclists, horses and carts and the people waiting. What was it they were waiting for? The road rose and fell in a straight cut between sugar plantations. The dense forests of leaves swayed high above the sun-blackened skin of workers in straw hats bent over their machetes. The verges were littered with stringy bits of flattened brown cane. After a few miles, we turned left over a railway line and into the courtyard of a mansion house. Through the windscreen the base of a tower was visible. I climbed out of the car, and the heat which I thought we'd left back in town pressed down on me. As I stood up, my head reflexed backwards to take in the unexpected height of the tower. Like a ridiculous travesty of a wedding cake, it rose, tier upon tier into the hot white cloud. I felt slightly sick.

'What is it? Or was it?'

'For the rich master. He use to watch his slaves.'

'Slaves?'

'*Si amiga.*' He picked up my hand and started to pull me towards it. 'Come. We climb.'

The custodian at the bottom looked at us both and then spoke to me in English. I paid a dollar for each of us then we started to clatter up the wooden staircases. They swayed. I wondered if there was such a thing as health and safety regulations.

'Is it much further?' I asked when Antonio waited for me after three staircases.

'*Poca mas.* A few more.' And he sprung upwards on flip-flop feet.

At last we stood in the arched window of the summit, leaning on a sturdy metal grille. I wanted to sit down. Sweat trickled down the inside of both my legs underneath my shorts. Way below I saw the car. Antonio's friend was now sitting on it, leaning back on straight arms, his legs splayed around the silver swan which crested the bonnet. He was surrounded by a small group of girls in micro-length shorts. Something white worked in their hands as they chatted. Even at that distance you could see that they had the poise of all young women here. Heads high, backs arched to push the shoulders back and the boobs out. It had taken me a while to realize that the ones in skin-tight Lycra grafting themselves to the arms of fat foreign men were prostitutes. Even the ordinary girls had this belief in their bodies. But Antonio was with me. Not them.

A train whistled to our left and we could see it, dinky-style, almost making a bracelet as it curved between the sugar plantation and the cluster of white houses separated by lines of washing and shaded by the spread of mango trees.

'You like?'

'I like the view very much, Antonio.' I felt a surge of gratitude. Of well being. A man wanting to please me. 'Thank you for bringing me.' I was close to him, in that opposite kind of way. The fantasy trespassed into my waking mind. It would have been the simplest thing to make a bridge between us, to slide off my scarf, the red one, bright with flowers, and capture his neck in it. A simple step to pull his head down to mine. But we slipped sideways out of the possibility. Slipped without even scuffing each other's edges. He started back down the stairs.

As we came back out into the courtyard, the girls who had been around the car clustered around us. Now I could see that the white things in their hands were crocheted goods – tablecloths, shawls, napkins. They had a towel rack covered in them. A girl with the body of an athlete, her black hair whisked up in a baseball cap and wearing bright white trainers pushed to the front and spoke to me, gesturing at the cloths. She arranged one of the shawls around my shoulders, leaning over me with good-humoured murmurs to pat it in place.

'She ask you if you like to buy some textiles,' said Antonio, and stood back, away from the huddle. Just as the heat had pursued me, I felt oppressed by the girls and their cloths, the way they flicked their smiles between me and Antonio and waved the cloths near to my face. There was a sickly smell of something – coconut perhaps. Why didn't Antonio tell them to leave me alone? I pulled at the heavy shawl on my shoulders and pushed it at the girl in the baseball cap, knocking my way through the towel rack and out of the huddle towards the car.

'Hey, *amiga*. What's wrong?' I heard Antonio call after me. 'You don't want any? Very special to this place.'

• • • • • • • • • • • • • • • • • • •

When I looked back from the safety of the back seat of the car, he was shaking dust off the cloths and returning them to the rack. The baseball girl was flashing her hands and upper body at him but he shrugged and backed off towards the car.

I was hanging my head when he climbed in next to me on the back seat. Tears of frustration, heat and shame were ready to burst out of me.

'I'm sorry. I didn't mean anything,' I said, my head still bowed.

'That one.' He nodded his head towards the baseball girl. 'She my sister. Is hard for us. Our father is ill. We have to try to make money.'

I looked up at him. Of course. That was why we were here. Nothing to do with any attraction. Not even friendship. The stupid old woman in me thudded back down to earth. I waved goodbye to my fantasy. It was a bit sad really. That tugging at the edges of my subconscious had become quite familiar; like a friend.

I had to stifle a laugh when he passed a handkerchief to me. Mopping someone else's tears was a gesture I well recognized as a mother. But this was a mere boy, younger even than my own children.

I didn't use it for a while. I stared down at it, flat and folded in my hands. It was white. Very white. Folded neatly. Pressed, maybe. Was that the sort of whiteness you get from bleaching in the sun here or was it some poor girl with her knuckles rubbed red in a sink of cold water? His mother even? Oh God, maybe his wife. I opened the handkerchief and mopped my cheeks. Antonio looked at me with his head on one side. I thought to give him the handkerchief back, but then I saw as I dangled it from my hand that it had a smudge of my lipstick on it. And I don't suppose he would want my tears.

•   •   •   •   •   •   •   •   •   •   •   •   •   •   •   •   •   •

It felt more like a dance hall than a provincial bus station. We passed between the groups of travellers, towards the obvious huddle of westerners waiting for the tourist bus back to Havana. Salsa music goaded passion out of the crowd. Feet shuffled and pelvises rocked to the beat as people got on with the sociable business of waiting in the holding area before being squeezed onto the buses through a narrow gate. Crowd sweat warmed my nostrils. How was it that it wasn't an unpleasant smell here? It just smelt like an affirmation of living. As I squeezed through, I caught my handbag strap on the neck of a guitar projecting from an old man's back, and nearly pulled it to the floor. It triggered a chorus of laughter from him and his friends. He pulled the fat stub of a cigar from his mouth and waved it at me as he cackled.

Antonio and I found a small area of shade and leant against the rough concrete wall. Before I went through the gate, he kissed me. Once on each cheek. And I thought I caught a faint whiff of raw onion. I was looking forward to settling on the bus, starting to re-locate the right person in the right body. By the time I got to Gatwick I knew the transformation would be complete and Carol would never guess.

It was cool on the bus. I felt my skin begin to dry, to feel more like it did at home. I might even need a cardigan. He stood next to my window. The brightness of the pink t-shirt I'd bought him in the hotel shop was muted by the smoked glass. I mouthed as silently as I could, 'I'll write,' and mimicked scribbling with my hand. 'I won't forget the jeans.' After all they'd only cost about thirty five pounds. So my children tell me. He smiled. The bus started to pull away. He waved and smiled. Smiled and waved. As I put on my cardigan, I found his handkerchief was still in the pocket. No longer pressed and pristine. It was too late to give it back now. I let it dangle. And it felt like the right gesture. I waved the hanky at him through the window.

Once we were out of sight of the station and Antonio, I turned away from the window. Across the aisle from me was a woman of Carol's age. Her legs had been sun and sandblasted to mahogany on the beach. She was looking at me. She turned away as she saw me register it. I thought I saw disgust on her face. I smiled and looked back out of my own window.

Zero Woman

As she walked home down Drake Street, Sylvia saw an odd-looking man heading for the corner shop. She hadn't seen him before. He was shuffling along like a foot-bound Chinese girl. Each step seemed to anticipate the bruise from the obstacle it was going to run into. There was a greyish look to all his clothes. He was so bent over, apparently studying the ground, that as they passed each other, the crown of his grey head greeted her. Unlike her other neighbours, who seemed to drive everywhere, he at least used the pavement. But with that posture he wasn't likely to notice her any more than they did.

She closed herself into the hall, behind her maroon Georgian door. Despite moving into number forty-one several days ago, she'd met none of her neighbours yet. Not that she had much desire to be friendly anyway. All that cup-of-sugar stuff. So facile, and it led to no good. They had good reason to ignore her. She knew that her severe look, with her hooded eyes and her paleness put her work colleagues off. They let her keep her head down while they cackled over the photocopier. And these days, now that she'd given up dyeing it, there was her short grey hair. She'd succumbed to the colour of obscurity, despite the young person she felt was still inside her, waving hopelessly at the portholes of a sinking ship. 'Excuse me,' she felt like yelling out, through the walls to her neighbours, to the street, the town, the universe, to anyone prepared to listen. 'Excuse me. I'm still here!'

Sylvia had become quite invisible as she crept towards old age. Ironically, it reminded her of being very young, seven or eight years old, when her mother had taken her to buy a riding hat for a birthday present. They were all huge for her except for the size zero which fitted perfectly. She couldn't understand how her head felt so real to her, quite large really, certainly capable of filling the satin-lined cup shape of a hat. And yet it was nothing. That was how she felt now; she had become Zero Woman.

After she'd taken off her coat and made a cup of tea, Sylvia wondered what to do next. Before her daughter had left home for university and stopped returning home even in her holidays, there'd always been something. Cooking, tidying, a spot of nagging or teenage counselling. Sylvia's life had been full for so long, almost too full, with her job as a financial administrator and a house and daughter to run. She'd craved some sort of change. A new job was unrealistic – another company wouldn't have her at her age. The previous house was much too big for her alone. So the move to the suburb was her new start. Or perhaps, as she was discovering, it was going to be more like her disappearance.

• • • • • • • • • • • • • • • • • •

She left the house in the morning, as Drake Street was rocked by extremes of commotion and stillness. Doors crashed open and shut as women trailed children, screams and bags into the open jaws of their cars. Smoked glass and air conditioning closed around them and spirited them off somewhere. Sylvia walked on towards the station, slowing a little outside number fifteen where they did B&B. She enjoyed the smell of bacon and eggs which hung in the air around the open windows, and the way it mingled with the exotic azalea scents in the front garden.

Drake Street was dominated by parked cars. Nose to tail on each side of the road. It was as if they were waiting for something. They pushed towards some sort of crisis at the end of the street, and they shone and glistened with money and attention. She'd had a car once. She'd even gone places in it.

She noticed the Polo because it *didn't* glisten. It had obviously once been red, but a sticky layer of sap from the overhanging lime trees had given it a greenish overlay, as if it was growing a light mould. The windscreen wipers were weighed down with dead leaves and sweet wrappers. Large paws had been applied like potato prints in a primary school classroom to make random patterns of dust on the sticky bonnet. The tyres were squarish under the weight of the car.

Sylvia stopped to look more closely. She peered in through the windscreen. It was hard to see through the sap and filth. There were two empty Evian water bottles on the passenger seat; a Twix wrapper had oozed a finger of chocolate onto the dashboard. She stooped down to look in the side windows. Her fingers came away from the roof with a print of black; sticky and powdery at the same time. A dried-up teabag festered in the footwell with some dirty paintbrushes. Yellowing newspapers were scattered across the back seat with an Ordnance Survey map of the Lake District, a Daler sketchpad, a single training shoe. Sylvia imagined glorious days of motoring; the Polo transporting pioneering spirits and picnic baskets to the countryside. Now it was down-at-heel and forgotten. She looked around at the houses nearest to the car for a clue to the ownership. But numbers twenty-nine and thirty-one, twenty-eight and thirty opposite, stared blankly back.

Something about the abandoned car worried her. Had the owner been taken ill? Was he or she dead? Some poor single soul who everyone had forgotten, rotting away after a heart attack and not discovered until the first heat of the summer trickled the evidence under the door and onto the street.

●　●　●　●　●　●　●　●　●　●　●　●　●　●　●　●

Most of the residents of Drake Street had paved their front gardens, some around a straggly rose bush or hydrangea. The unpaved ones were surprisingly neglected and overgrown, and one was chaotic with discarded kitchen containers. Her neighbours reserved their attentions for their back gardens. Sylvia could see, by peeking through the gaps between houses, that lupins, buddleia and sweet peas spilt gloriously around their back lawns. She wasn't much of a gardener herself and wasn't about to start filling her time with it. Gardening could get obsessive. Sometimes it seemed as if a law had condemned everyone to spend Sundays on their hands and knees scrabbling in their herbaceous borders. It was repressive – Amnesty International should take a position on it. She might even write a letter.

One day she arrived home to a parcel on her front door mat. A long leather whip uncoiled out of foreign newspaper. Her sister, Joan, had brought it back for her from Tunisia. 'Fine local leatherwork', the attached leaflet said. But what was she supposed to do with it? She took it into the middle of her lawn where she was surrounded by an overgrown mass of dead foliage – the desiccated flowers that scolded her when she was washing up at the kitchen window. She should deadhead them, painstakingly, one at a time, but had no intention of doing so.

She flicked her arm back and swung the whip. It cracked around her, and transformed from soft leather to the sharpest of knives. She flicked it again and was shocked to hear a yelp slipping cowboyish out of her mouth. A line seemed to have formed through the whip and her arm, to a creature buried inside her. It was like a crustacean, a mussel maybe, peering out of the jaws of its newly opening shell. Then she realized that she was gardening. At a certain height they flew off – those wretched dried up heads of roses and ox-eye daisies. She didn't even need to move. This was her sort of gardening. The neighbours weren't interfering. No approaching sirens warned of the onset of her insanity. And her daughter's embarrassed glares were out of the equation. An hour or so later, cries of 'off with their heads' were still punctuating her thoughts as the suburban dusk settled over Drake Street.

• • • • • • • • • • • • • • • • • • •

She got to know the Polo well as her new daily routine to and from work became established. She passed it twice a day, noting that it hadn't moved, noting new things about it such as the ragged end of the aerial where it had been snapped off, a trail of dog pee making a black line down the tyres. On most mornings the car had a resident. A large ginger cat graced the bonnet; sitting perfectly central, enthroned on the poop of the car like one of those carved figures on the front of old ships. It was proud and erect, paws curled inwards in front of its broad white chest, staring directly ahead. It gave the car a look of dynamism. Leading the voyage; bringing the travellers luck; its sights fixed on a distant destination. The cat believed the Polo was going somewhere. Sylvia liked that.

She decided to ask the Grey Man about the car when she passed him again. Perhaps he would know something about it. She didn't really want to get caught up with an oddball, but they did already have a certain intimacy, as they appeared to share the sole use of the pavement. However, when they did pass again, and she slowed a bit and coughed, hoping to interrupt his scrutiny of the cracks in the pavement, he simply shuffled on past, twisting a glance up to her through heavy glasses when he got level with her feet.

• • • • • • • • • • • • • • • • • •

On Saturday night she took herself out for a treat. At the end of the road, next to the corner shop, was an Italian restaurant. As she had suspected, it was one of those fake ones, with all the names but none of the bustle and glamour of the real thing. She sat at a table in the window and chose from the menu. The waiter was draping himself from an elbow propped on a high shelf, a white tea towel flung over one of his shoulders. He was engrossed with the barmaid who had her back to Sylvia. They looked to be kids straight out of school with stick insect legs and white teeth.

Sylvia was hungry and thirsty. She waited. Nothing happened except that pizza aroma meandered towards her from other tables. The waiter and barmaid remained gripped by mutual fascination, unaware of her nods and smiles in their direction.

The menu was a long cream card, printed tastefully in brown ink. An experiment occurred to Sylvia. Her hand colluded with her inner creature. She held a corner of the menu to the candle flame. It lit well. The card was good combustible material, and the flames started to lick down the edge, galloping past the antipastos, the main courses, and finally down to the sweets. It only had the beverages to go when the waiter's neck suddenly appeared long over the head of the barmaid, and he pushed past her, heading for Sylvia's table. She was triumphant. She dipped the menu in and out of her jug of water, and consulted it, dripping carbon-coloured drops onto the white tablecloth.

'For starters, smoked salmon crostini, followed by parmigiano freddo pizza. Not too much tomato.' She smiled up at the waiter. 'A dish of marinated olives and a half carafe of rioja.' She held out the dripping menu to him and he hesitated before taking a corner of it between thumb and forefinger and stomping back towards the kitchen.

•   •   •   •   •   •   •   •   •   •   •   •   •   •   •   •   •   •

As she returned home past the Polo, the Grey Man was at the door of number twenty-nine. His head was bent in its usual way and he was rustling a carrier bag, looking for something. Sylvia heard small murmurs of frustration emanating from him. She had a chance to study his greyness a little more. It was particularly pronounced over his shoulders. She suspected that a build up of dandruff was obscuring the original dark colour of his suit. The trousers were too short and he wore odd coloured socks. A wave of revulsion buffeted her. Then the rustling stopped and she saw his hand shaking the key towards the door. She heard the clatter as the keys hit the ground and he stooped to pick them up, bending awkwardly with knees and back and patting the ground around his feet until he felt the metal. His garden path was lined on each side with a jumble of paint tubs, yoghurt pots, margarine containers, all bursting with plants – geraniums and fuschias and marigolds and so on. She couldn't imagine anyone wanting to go to so much trouble just for plants. As the Grey Man moved crab-like on the path, a rush of colour darted across the road and into his garden. The big ginger cat curled around his calves and pointed its nose up towards his face.

'Hello, Jimmy. Hello, Jimmy.' She heard the Grey Man mumble. 'I'm coming, just hang on, can't you?'

So the Grey Man was the cat owner. She pictured the cat curled up on his lap, in front of the TV, or by the glow of an electric bar fire.

• • • • • • • • • • • • • • • •

Sylvia gradually became friendly with the cat. He was already on his poop as she brushed through the cobweb traps which laced across the pavement each morning. A soft creature with spiky whiskers and a chip out of one ear. She thought of him as the Ship's Cat. He began to accept her clucks and strokes. In the morning she was in too much of a rush, but in the evenings, she'd stop for a moment by the car. She enjoyed the brush of his thick greasy fur on her fingers and the fishy smell of his miaow. Sometimes he would arch his back towards her hand, and she felt flattered – he responded to her. It became a regular thing. The Ship's Cat became like a friend, almost. But he always darted off to greet the Grey Man when he came shuffling along. His real love.

Her relationship with the cat also pressed her into action on the car. One day she put a small bottle of water and a J-cloth into her briefcase. On her way home, she fumbled them out onto the bonnet. She swiped the cloth over a portion of the windscreen with one hand, while she stroked the cat with the other. She felt like a fairy godmother, making a patch of clean glass appear from under the grime.

She developed a daily routine; became more dedicated. Her stops by the car became longer, less surreptitious. After all, no one had complained. If she stopped to ask herself why she stood her briefcase on the pavement and splashed and polished and scrutinized the car, all in her office clothes, her only answer was the pleasure she felt as she rubbed the shabbiness and the smell of decay away from each portion. And perhaps she had a vague fantasy that one day she would sit proudly in the driver's seat, sparkling in the sunshine, heading for an adventure, wearing a pair of elegant string and tan leather driving gloves. Going somewhere.

She started to use a sponge rather than a J-cloth and bought some turtle wax shampoo that did the job in no time according to the ads in the Sunday paper. Sometimes she was there for as long as ten minutes, until the sponge became too dirty to continue. Before long, the entire bonnet had been reclaimed from its green haze. It was tomato red again. And it shone.

The cat supervised her. He looked a little unsure on the newly slippery surface at first, recoiling from the shampoo smell as if something had nipped his nose. Sylvia fancied he could see his reflection in the bonnet, and was enjoying his residence being upgraded. He always settled back down in the same poop place. She had to wipe away his paw prints from the bonnet every day before she started on the next uncharted territory; the side panels, doors, rear windscreen.

She still had no idea who the car belonged to, but it didn't really seem to matter. It had started to feel like hers as much as anyone's. That was, until a particularly warm and sunny evening tempted her to spend longer than usual on her task. She was excited by the emerging gleam on the door handles and the petrol cap as she worked away with chrome polish on a cloth. These were the finishing touches, the job was nearly done. She dodged the traffic to stand in the middle of the road, hands on hips, to admire how it shone in the sun.

A flash of light from somewhere nearby distracted her. As she glanced up to locate the source, it flashed again, and this time it came clearly from the front window of number twenty-nine. She found herself staring straight into two small circles of light. They puzzled her, so she kept staring. When her eyes adjusted to the relative dark of the room behind them, she realized that they were attached at eye level to a shadowy figure. As she watched, the circles of light moved and vanished and she could see clearly the outline of a man, looking out, with something in his hands. Something that she now recognized as a pair of binoculars. The lenses had caught the sun, as it sank towards the roofs opposite. That was the flash. The Grey Man had been watching her.

She hid her confusion by squeezing the remainder of the chrome polish on to her cloth and returning to the task. It was less enjoyable now, with the unfamiliar feeling of being watched. Someone noticing she was there, when perhaps she shouldn't be. It must be his car then. It was parked more or less outside his house, after all. How often had he watched her without her realizing? Maybe since she first started it. But he was a grown man. If he objected to her improving it, he could have come out and told her. It was he who had let it get into this state in the first place. He was obviously a weirdo, spying on everyday folk like this. Nevertheless she decided to call it a day, gathered up her things without looking back towards his window, and went home to find something else to do.

•   •   •   •   •   •   •   •   •   •   •   •   •   •   •   •   •

She had to make a final blitz on the car, despite the knowledge that she'd been discovered. It was so nearly complete, just the hub caps to go. But they were black with grease and would need more than ten minutes with a damp cloth. She would have to be discreet. She got up at first light on the Saturday, put on her wellies and waterproof coat, and filled a bucket with hot water and the turtle stuff. No one was around. The bucket was heavy and the water sloshed onto the pavement with each step.

When she got to the car, it looked slightly different – something hard to define. The windows weren't as transparent as they had been, they were misted with light condensation on the inside. When she peered through them, it was clear that someone had been inside the car. All the rubbish had been replaced with pots of plants and seedlings bursting out of black compost, compost that was spilled in sooty patches on the seats. The pots were spread across the back shelf, on the back seat, even propped along the dashboard and in the door pockets. It was obvious who had put them there.

Sylvia pressed on regardless, as she was working against the clock. The Ship's Cat sat on the pavement while she scrubbed the grime off the hub caps. Finally, she stood in her wellies and admired the car from each angle. It was gloriously red and shiny. The picture was complete. The car could take pride in its place on the street. It was redeemed from obscurity. Her triumph, the slight choke in her throat, was spoilt a bit by the feeling that the car wasn't 'hers' any more. And she certainly wouldn't be going anywhere in it now that it had become a greenhouse. The adventure was at an end.

While she was admiring it, the Ship's Cat ran towards the opening door of number twenty-nine. Sylvia froze as the Grey Man shuffled towards her down the garden path carrying more plant pots and a watering can. She saw the questioning frown above his squint when he got close to her and straightened up.

'Hello,' he said.

Sylvia was trapped between him and the car, her arms too occupied with the heavy bucket to get away. He walked around her to the driver's door which he opened with a key. He bent himself into the car, found a place for the new pots, and checked for growth and soil moisture in the existing ones.

Sylvia noticed how his trousers rode up his legs as he bent forward. The odd socks were at half-mast. Her hands flickered with the idea of emptying her bucket. Emptying it now, while his feet were in the gutter in nice absorbent plimsolls. But he backed out and faced her again too soon.

'Courgettes are doing nicely,' he said.

'It's yours then. I didn't know.'

'I've always wanted a greenhouse. Never thought of the car having another use until I saw you giving it some attention.' He combed a hand through his grey forelock, leaving clods of compost peppered in it. 'I can't drive anymore you see. My eyes.' He tapped at his glasses.

She nodded. His voice surprised her; it sounded too bright to fit his appearance, too normal. He was like a crab, transforming between beach and restaurant with its pink succulent flesh inside the ugly shell. She was still foolishly attached to the full bucket. She took it to a nearby drain and upended it so the water leapt back at her and then gurgled away. Now she could move more easily, she would go home.

'I'm very grateful,' he said.

'Sorry?'

'That you made me notice it. Here – this is for you.' He held out a pot.

'Thank you.' She had no idea what the plant was. It had big fleshy leaves that looked like they could spike you and a high central bud about to burst into flower. What would she want with a plant with all its messy soil and needing looked after and so on?

'Wonderful displays,' he touched the bud. 'It'll be even better next year. Put it in a nice sunny spot. It needs to get into the soil.' He smiled at her. 'I grew it from seed.'

She put the pot in her empty bucket and glanced around at the car. It really looked something, complete with its Ship's Cat crest. She walked over and ran a hand down his ginger fur. He arched his back up to her. He was still her friend, even if she had finished with the car.

'Well, enjoy your ... greenhouse.'

'I will, I will.'

●　●　●　●　●　●　●　●　●　●　●　●　●　●　●　●　●

She carried the plant through the house to the back garden and abandoned it there. It wasn't until she was washing up the next evening that she thought about it. The top of the spiky bud was nodding in the breeze, summoning her. She went out and faced it, hands on hips.

'OK,' she said. 'You win.' Then she went and found a trowel in her shed, and dug a hole in the border, pushing back the weeds that threatened to engulf the newcomer. The soil felt warm and crumbly on her hands. It reminded her of the Grey Man, ridiculous with compost stuck in his hair.

She stood back when she'd finished and admired her handiwork. The plant stood proud among the weeds. Maybe tomorrow she'd clear some of them. And she could get some other plants to grow in their place, though she had no idea what sort or where to get them from. Maybe she could ask the Grey Man for some advice, although she realized she hadn't even asked him his name, nor told him hers.

She filled a jug with water in the kitchen and trickled it around the roots of the plant.

The Fall

Jim was spread-eagled over the bonnet of the car with the open map. He pinned the edges down hard with his palms. Marjorie held her face up to the early morning sun and waited, her small rucksack already on her back. She gazed at the mountains and hummed. Something light and tuneless. Humming was good for that – filling the spaces, taking your mind off other things. She was only vaguely aware of doing it. It was her family who'd forced her to realize, after all three grown-up children had trailed her around the house making dying bee noises. 'The Humbug' they called her.

'See, it'll be much quicker this way,' Jim said. Marjorie didn't bother responding. Likely as not he wasn't really talking to her; briefing himself for the expedition.

'Don't you want to see where we're going?' He cranked his neck round to see her.

'OK, love.' And she put a hand on one of his shoulders and leant over too, towards the map. 'Show me what I'm in for then.' Maps were not Marjorie's forte. There were green bits for trees, blue bits for lochs; she understood that. But all those lines and squiggles. Well.

'See, we'd have to go all the way around there.' He drew an arc with his finger along a dotted line.

A path, then. 'Yes?'

'When we can just go straight up here.' His finger stabbed a short distance through a cluster of irregular concentric circles. He looked up at her, smiling, triumphant.

'And what are those amoeba things?'

'Amoebas?'

'Those squiggly circle things.' She pointed at the concentric circles.

'Marjorie.' He put one hand up to the back of her neck and swivelled her gaze in the direction of his pointing finger. 'See those high pointy things? You've come across one or two in your time?' She nodded. 'Well on the map they turn into contours and look like "squiggly circle things".' He peered into her face to make sure she was following. '"Hills". They're sometimes known as "hills".'

'Ah,' she said. 'Thanks, Jim. It's ringing a bell now.'

He cuffed the back of her head. A sprinkle of raindrops tapped on to the map from an apparently clear sky.

'Better not get the map wet,' she said. And he folded it back into its plastic wallet.

• • • • • • • • • • • • • • • • • •

'Are you sure about this route?' Marjorie said to Jim's back a little later. He was already laying the trail towards the sheer face of the hill. The terrier, Bobby, clung to his heels, nose down, tail up. Marjorie had stopped to stuff a jumper into her rucksack. At first she thought he hadn't heard, but after a few more strides, he stopped and turned back to her. She thought she saw something dart behind his eyes, like a goldfish in a dirty tank.

'It's just that it looks steep. Too steep,' she said. He turned away from her again to look at the hill. Jim and Bobby stood next to each other. Marjorie was amused by their similarities; they seemed to imitate each other. Short legs planted slightly apart; noses upwards sniffing the challenge. A solid pair. But Jim didn't pant. Of course not.

'It'll be fine. It's much quicker this way. I showed you – remember?'

She picked up her rucksack, mentally re-packing the small parcel she always carried on hill-walking trips. The Jim-is-always-right parcel. It was compact and durable. Like the first aid kit that they carried in a Tupperware box containing essential treatments for cuts, strains and insect bites and which they re-stocked religiously from the bathroom cupboard. The Jim-is-always-right parcel allowed them both to feel confident. After all, it was so much easier to let Jim take this role; to trust him. True enough, in the early years of their marriage she had fought it a bit. And it hadn't been just about walking. There was the choice of schools for the children, the best pension scheme to buy into, even what sort of dog to have (Marjorie always wanted a collie). But the painful negotiations died down as they settled into their married life. A collie really was too big in a suburban house, she accepted that now.

Marjorie relaxed, the parcel safely back in her rucksack.

'It always looks steeper than it really is, remember?' he called over his shoulder as they set off again. He was right. Going up *and* down. Like when they'd stood on the Aonach Eagach ridge in Glencoe, their senses tumbled in deep sea mist. A chink in the cloud had framed the silver line of the river and tourist cars in the glen below, and he'd said, 'We can go down here,' and pointed at a slope of impossibly sheer scree. She shrugged and followed after a few protestations, and they scrambled down, breaking into smiles as they joined the sunshine and day-trippers in the glen.

She was almost reckless in her trust. She had to admit, Jim extended her, forced her into situations she wouldn't have put herself in. Friends were amazed by her escapades.

At their joint retirement party a few weeks earlier, Marjorie had stood, embraced by a circle of her teacher friends, tearing at wrapping paper on a small gift.

'I'll be able to find my way to the shops now, anyway,' she laughed. 'Look Jim, I'll be able to find my way to the shops.' She beckoned him over from the bar and took his sandwich in exchange for the compass. He turned it over.

'It's a good one, that. A very good one.' They swapped back again.

'Thanks, girls,' she hugged them one at a time.

'Maybe I should learn to use it now I've got all this time on my hands. What do you reckon, Jim. Will you get bored with being my guiding light?'

'Never, my darling. Not until I drop dead with that heart attack on the hill.' He retreated towards the bar with his sandwich.

'I suppose I ought to know which direction to carry you in,' she called after him. She turned back to her friends. 'Though I have a feeling a ghostly voice will shout directions through the clouds.' A smirk passed silently around the circle of faces.

•   •   •   •   •   •   •   •   •   •   •   •   •   •   •   •   •   •

She followed Jim and Bobby on gently rising ground towards the hulk of the hill. Bedclothes of cloud unravelled from a peak, allowing it to stretch up into the bright morning. She sucked in a lungful of air and stretched her arms over her head. She was like Julie Andrews, tripping weightlessly through mountain meadows studded with wild flowers. She had to recognize her limitations though. She might be a little over-stretched by trying to sing and look beautiful as well.

There was joy in following, she decided. Not taking the responsibility meant she didn't have to think. She just luxuriated in the sensations. She mentally caressed the flowers, naming the ones she knew – tormentil, heath bedstraw – and trying to avoid walking on the orchids. Patches of black moss were silken and moleskin under her fingers. Reeds pricked her bare calves. Her steps flicked frogs out of the squelch. The rocks were decorated with lichens – antique white and green. And some had tendrils that reached out into the air, like corals escaped from *The Underwater World of Jacques Cousteau*. She stretched her arms in front of her, swum a few breaststrokes through the air. Why not? No one was there to see. Certainly not Jim, way up ahead with no idea of the fun she was having.

It was getting steeper, and she felt the warm grate of rock on her hands as she pulled herself up. The wind increased as they got higher, lifting the hair away from her face. Her lungs started to hurt, and Julie Andrews faded to black and white. Marjorie stopped to draw breath. Jim was up ahead, standing on a ledge. He was pushed vertical by a rock in front of his chest. His arms were spread open to hold himself to it. His head twitched to left and right, looking for the next part of his route. They were scrambling now, not walking.

Marjorie followed Jim and Bobby into a gully to the right where they continued upwards, sheltered on both sides by moss and rock. Ferns sprouted from a gurgle and spout of water, unseen under the rocks in the deepest part of the gully. Her boots slipped on the wet surface. Despite the shelter, she understood why Jim moved back to the left, onto the drier, but more exposed rocks. She didn't look down, followed Bobby along a wide ledge. Jim was above them, but neither she nor Bobby could see how to follow him. She stopped, faced the rock, leant into it.

Jim looked down and said something that the wind lifted away from her and then, 'You stay there. I'll go and look around the corner. Find the best way.' Grey-bottomed clouds lumbered between Jim's head and the sun, flattening and blackening the peaks and corries around them. The sparkle disappeared from the straight white lines of waterfalls. The rock started to cool under her hands. She didn't feel like moving anyway.

Jim levered himself upwards until he knelt at the next level. Then he stood up and disappeared from view. Bobby trotted to and fro next to Marjorie, looking upwards for a way to follow, rocking back onto his haunches every now and again to look higher, front paws lifting off the ground.

'Stay here, Bobby,' Marjorie said. Her voice was like a wisp of something tossed in the wind. The dog ignored her. He hurtled up at the ledge where he'd seen Jim disappear. His front paws caught the lip of the rock, and she heard his extended claws scrabble against it, saw the urge of his head and neck upwards, before he peeled backwards, swivelling into a roll of fur that carried him down. Past Marjorie. Down.

She let out a low wail. Bobby. Indestructible Bobby. Her eyes followed him downwards and one of her knees started to beat a rhythm against the rock in front of her. Several feet below, Bobby's paws found purchase on another ledge. He scrambled upright. Shook himself. Under his fringe, he rolled his eyes up towards Marjorie without moving his head. One of his 'did-she-notice?' gestures. He was embarrassed. That was all.

'Are you OK Bobby?' she shouted over the wind, leaning down to see him. Then her senses lurched and swayed. As he bounded upwards by another route, she refocused. Off Bobby, onto what was beyond him. She saw a sheep. Far below. Directly below. Like the speck she suddenly felt herself, pinned against a rock face. She'd climbed all that way. So far up. And she could fall all that way. Rolling and bouncing like Bobby. Except she was heavier, would have more momentum.

She reached deeper above the rock with her hands, gripped the rough heather stems. As if they would save her. The thing was to stay still. Jim would come back with a solution. He'd find an easy way, just out of sight; a staircase, even an escalator. Wouldn't he? She waited. Clung to the rock. Stared into its lined face. Heard the insane whine of her own humming. And below her, above her, inside her, time contracted and expanded. A tide went way, way out. And she thought about Jim moving away from her around the corner. Had his shoulders looked less robust than in the old days? Were there other hints she should have been taking?

•   •   •   •   •   •   •   •   •   •   •   •   •   •   •   •   •   •

A boot scuffed into sight above her. Coming down. And then Bobby's whiskery face appeared crouched between paws, one of them bloody. They both joined her on her ledge. She continued to cling. Jim's sweat-smell, the heat he seemed to project, enveloped the three of them like a familiar mist. She stopped shivering. Waited to know what would happen next.

'It's loose rock,' Jim said. 'Too dangerous when it's this steep. We'll have to go down.'

'Down?' Marjorie stared at him. Down. All that way back to the tiny sheep. Across the mass of contours he'd shown her on the map. It was horrible going down on steep ground, feeling backwards for footholds you couldn't see.

'Sorry, love.' He seemed to avoid her eyes. 'We'll take it slowly. I'll lead you.' She continued to stare at him until his eyes were forced to meet hers. It reminded her of Bobby's look earlier. Yes, she thought. I *did* notice. She grew braver. Turned on the ledge so that she faced Jim rather then the rock. Felt the vastness below her on one side. She wasn't clinging any more.

And then it happened. The fall came as she knew it would. She saw the compact parcel she had carried all those years fall out of her rucksack. Tumble like the dog. But this time it crashed on downwards, bouncing off rocks, displacing lumps of bog, scattering sheep in its radius. The contents were displayed across the hillside, messy and embarrassing, like a rubbish bag pulled apart on the street for neighbours to see. It took several minutes for everything to settle. For her to see the hillside clearly again. To feel a thrill at the devastation.

She let him lead her down. Slow and meticulous. Accepted his instructions.

'A bit further to your left, love,'

'A small stretch more.'

She heard his questions, 'Are you OK?' and the reassurances, 'You're doing fine. We're nearly there.' And she didn't question; knew that they were safe.

When they got to the bottom and were back on the firm path that led to the car, she walked in front. And her rucksack felt light on her back.

The second wish

A couple of days after he received the card, George started to compose the letter he would write to his son. He sat in his armchair by the French windows and let his eyes rest on the azaleas while he mulled over what he really wanted to say. It had been a long time, but at least now the letter wouldn't be difficult to begin.

Dear Mark,

Getting Yvonne's card knocked the legs out from under me. The photo fell on the floor and when I picked it up, there you were, the three of you. I could tell from the bed rail and drip in the background that mother and baby were still in the hospital when it was taken. It took me back to a similar scene thirty odd years ago. And I thought, son, this is daft, I should write and tell you. Why don't we bury the hatchet? Let's face it, it's been too long lying in the weather, getting blunt and rusty.

I couldn't settle to anything after I got the card so I took a walk to the wishing tree. I wonder if you remember us going there together when you were small? I hung a charm in the tree for the little boy (I don't know his name, just that he weighed in at eight pounds, two ounces). I used a strip of material from some curtains I'd brought here from the old house but didn't need. Your mother made them. It felt right, the family association.

Did you know I built this house with my own hands? Of course it was retiring so soon after your mother died. Time was the one thing I did have. It kept me busy and I needed that. But now it's finished with every last fixture and fitting chosen and put in place by yours truly. I got some of the pictures of old RAF planes out of my archive and had them blown up, framed, and now they hang on my sitting room wall. I've got a desk to write letters at and some roses to prune and a lawn to mow. You wouldn't recognize me in my quiet cul-de-sac (it's only a stone's throw from the motorway but you'd never know). I'm quite the domesticated old man now.

The visits to the wishing tree started because Mark overhead a story his mother told while sharing coffee and toddler blues in a friend's kitchen one morning. It was about a childless woman who fastened a red ribbon onto the branches of the wishing tree and fell pregnant soon afterwards. Some fascination pulled Mark's eyes up from the pile of Lego on the floor to the adult faces.

'What's the wishing tree?' he interrupted. They ignored him until he screamed, 'Tell me, what is it? What is it?'

Beth turned briefly. 'It's just a tree where you go to make a wish about something very important that you want to come true.' She turned back to lock heads with her friend, to go onto the girl's caesarean and the departure of her husband soon after the birth.

A few weeks before Christmas he pestered her to go. Needing them both out of the house to get Sunday lunch ready, Beth encouraged him to pull his father out from under the newspaper. They went off hand in hand, Mark tripping small steps to keep up with his father down the muddy track.

George wasn't sure how easy the tree would be to find, but it was obvious. The track led right to it, past a pool sludgy with winter water lilies. There was a tree in the centre of a clearing, enclosed by larger trees. It was still and peculiarly quiet there. The branches splayed out, decorated with bows and tassels, like be-ribboned hair. Most of the cloth charms were faded by sunlight and weather, rotting. The more recent ones were still bright and hopeful.

George had to hold Mark up so he could reach the branches with his clumsy fingers. His breathing hardened and his face twisted with concentration. When George lowered him to the ground he wiped away the mud that Mark's wellies had left on his jacket and took the boy's hand, thinking homewards of gravy and Yorkshire pudding. But Mark was reluctant to move, staring upwards at his charm as it dangled among a mass of others. The sight triggered question after question:

'How will the person that collects the charms know that it's mine?'

'What if the wind blows it off, will my wish still work?'

'Will it work, Dad?'

George squatted down in front of the solemn figure to reassure him. As he smiled into Mark's face, he spotted a smear of honey on his son's cheek, left from breakfast. He resisted the urge to remove it with a neat lick of the tongue and instead took out a handkerchief from his coat pocket, licked a corner and rubbed the honey away.

'There you go, my honey monster,' he said. 'It's oozing out from all those beehives you keep in there, isn't it?' He knocked his knuckles on Mark's forehead. Face to face, eye to eye, the attention warmed a grin onto Mark's face, his eyes under the blonde fringe narrowing into mischief.

'I'm not a honey monster,' he shrieked, and George heard the giggles spilling from him as he ran ahead, back up the track. 'I'm a wishing monster, and I've got wishing hives in my head.'

Despite all the questions, Mark never revealed his wish, knowing what happens to wishes which aren't kept secret. Luckily, George and Beth had a good instinct for the way his mind worked and knew which plastic packages lured him to the toy shop shelves. He was rarely disappointed.

For a few years it was an annual tradition. When the TV ads had done their work, Mark put on his wellies and dragged George from his armchair. However, as he moved on to secondary school and more mature wishes for football strips and record players for Christmas, he adopted a more direct approach: hint; request; demand; sulk. The trips to the wishing tree became a thing of the past.

I don't know if you and Yvonne ever did get married. It doesn't matter to me now, but of course I'd like to know. I think your address is different from the one I had back then. I wonder what sort of place 'Reevie Mill' is and whether it's a town or a village you're in. I don't know that part of the world. And will Yvonne have given up her career for motherhood? Women amaze me these days, they seem to be taking over every kind of job. I never thought I'd see a woman fighter pilot I must say. They'll be wanting to be Santa Claus next, getting reindeer pilots' licences and growing long white beards.

I don't mean that against Yvonne of course. It was good of her to let me know about the boy.

They called in unexpectedly when Mark was first sharing a flat with Yvonne after finishing university. They just happened to be in town and thought it would be fun to see the young couple in their new nest. They waited on the doorstep for a long time after knocking. Their arms were full of Marks and Spencer's potted plants and a Dundee fruitcake. Barely able to hear each other over the yap of a dog inside, they heard it hurl all four furious paws against the door. Then it went silent.

'Must have winded itself,' said Beth.

'Catching it's breath before it starts with the battering ram,' said George. 'I didn't know they had a dog.' And then the yapping started up again.

Mark led them into a dark sitting room, with thin curtains still drawn against the daylight. A yellow electric guitar leaned against the wall, plugged into an amplifier, its red light glowing in the gloom. He'd obviously been engrossed in playing it when they arrived.

Yvonne wasn't in. To get to the sofa, George had to step over a pair of jeans on the floor, which lay in exactly the form they must have dropped from a body – the waist and fly round and gaping, the legs concertinaed beneath. They reminded George of a chrysalis. If the light hadn't been so dim, he might have seen the underpants still nestling inside, ready to spring out and embarrass him. He sensed that they belonged to a female.

They moved piles of music magazines off seats and Mark brought tins of beer which he and George drank with the cake. The small table which separated them was covered by a cloth which you could see glimpses of between the muddle of half burnt candles, a plectrum, a packet of cigarette papers, and several empty beer cans.

George tried not to look at the mess, just to concentrate on his son, but on the way home, he reached across the silence to say, 'That boy's a dead loss. He'll never grow up. No discipline.'

I wonder if you ever go hill walking now. We always had that in common, didn't we? Remember those days when you and I used to take the caravan to Scotland for a week, climb several hills in a day and then sit in a pub at night over maps and Mars Bars. I still go sometimes. There's a fellow across the road my sort of age enjoys it too. We had a weekend in the Lake District not long back. I'd like to think I passed on some of my navigational skills to you on those jaunts. I didn't spend forty years in the RAF not to know which direction I was going in. I don't know what else you inherited from me. Apart from my athlete's foot of course.

On the first summit they ate Wagon Wheels and looked at the view. It was hard to manage the wrappers with gloves on. They'd declared victory over their lungs and laggard legs to get there and George took satisfaction from the way their breath misted together in the cold air. A layer of cloud seemed to rest just above their heads, and below it, mountains and lochs spread out, russet with autumn and a source of sunshine hidden somewhere beyond the cloud.

The north-west wind soon filtered through their jumpers. George watched his son's face tighten, a young version of his own, the clamped jaw and stretched skin across the cheekbones showing the cold. He knew that look from the inside.

'Hey, I'm not taking you down the hill as a human ice-lolly. You'll make a sticky mess on the foot mat in the car when the heater comes on. And your Mum'll want to know what I did with the wrapper with the special offer on it.' George pulled the spare jumper from his rucksack. 'Here, put this on.'

'It's OK, I'm not cold, thanks.' Mark pulled his hat down further over his brow and turned away along the path.

By the time George had stuffed the jumper back into his rucksack and retied a bootlace, Mark was way down below, nearly on the col between the two summits, becoming as indistinct as the brown bush-shapes of deer grazing on the hill flanks around them. George followed him down and then along the rusty line of fence posts that led to the next summit. Even at fifteen, Mark was so much taller, with longer legs, fitter from playing sport at school. When George got to the top, Mark didn't turn from his slouch on the Ordnance Survey post. A can of coke was pressed to his lips.

'I like your team spirit, son. Vodka and coke is it?' He threw down his rucksack and sat on it. It had never cut him like this when Mark burst ahead on their wishing tree walks.

I see you with the boy in your arms. You'll be full of ambitions for him, watching him, recording his progress. Everyone seems to have camcorders these days – I would have done if they'd been invented in your young days. There'll be his first birthday, the first steps towards you, first

*steps away from you as he goes off to school, maybe even a
first mountain top. He's going to look like you, you can tell
from the photo even though he's so tiny. And who knows,
maybe there'll even be something of me about him too. Just
mind and keep his toes well dusted with fungicidal powder.*

He loved the feel of the small hot rasps of breath against his
neck when he held his one year old son in his arms. He
looked at their side-by-side faces in mirrors to see how the
shape of his son's eyes, nose, mouth, was reflected in his
own. The top of Mark's head rested just near lip height, and
he discovered in himself an instinct to kiss again and again
the young skull where the blonde hair curled and wisped.
And the head would rock back and the eyes rest on him.
Merry. That was how he thought of the look, a 'merry' look.
He savoured the smell of talc, baby lotion and milk,
nuzzling his face to his son for more.

It was at that time, just before communication
began through words that he felt most in love with his son.
Sometimes as he held him, a small fist would rise, the other
plugging thumb in mouth, and would grab a bit of stray
hair, an ear, a shirt collar. For minutes at a time he would
examine, explore, and scrutinize, with frowning eyes. And
then for no reason he'd cast a gurgle of laughter into his
father's face. George felt he was being explored and
discovered. It made him feel he existed. His form was
acknowledged in a way that it had never been before. He
became more aware of his own body, the hairs on his arms,
the veins in the back of his hands, the craggy skin around
his eyes. In the shower he noticed the shape of his limbs as
if for the first time. He liked himself more.

*I've probably never told you how I felt when you were born.
I don't know what I expected after all the months of
anticipation. Maybe a perfectly baked Victoria sponge, the
first groans of labour like the buzzer on the oven timer.
They cleaned and returned you to our arms and your*

mother and I came very close. I suddenly felt my place in the universe. In a flash it came, just as it had when I was about six and knew I was singing directly to God among the candles and the cathedral's high ceiling at my first carol service. I don't know why it's never been said before, but I felt you were part of me, an extension of my consciousness from that minute. You've been like my extra limb ever since. And by God, son, that extra limb makes me an awkward bastard to buy clothes for!

At the funeral reception, Mark and Yvonne stood with the decrepit Aunts and tear-stained neighbours. Yvonne's arm was through his, their heads inclining forward towards each other. He was uncomfortable in smart clothes, the tweed jacket too short on his long back, the tie already loosened. Every now and again Yvonne offered around the plate of canapés and vol-au-vents she was holding in the other hand.

Standing in the pool of sunlight the hotel's French windows threw in, George shook hands with parting guests and flourished a large white handkerchief around his nose and eyes. He was straight-backed in a dark suit whose legs were too long, crumpling slightly around the ankles. A taut line of awareness stretched across the room between him and his son. Their eyes never met and yet each was alive to the tension on the line as the other moved.

When the majority of the guests had left, Yvonne looked up into Mark's stooped face. 'You're going to have to speak to him, you know.'

Mark didn't answer but looked along the line that led to his father, seated opposite, face swallowed by a handkerchief in a shaking hand. He pushed out along the line, away from the canapés and Yvonne's protection.

'Dad?' But the handkerchief continued to bluster and shake, the eyes remaining hidden. Mark sank down into a squat so he was on eye level with his father. 'Dad, we have to leave soon, Yvonne and I. We've a long way to go.'

'Oh, you've always had a long way to go, my boy.' The handkerchief came down a bit. 'The whole blimmin' length of the Pan-American highway.' He shook his lowered head sideways, 'On roller skates.'

'OK, Dad.' Mark didn't react. 'Now's not the time to talk. Maybe we can get together later. You could come up and visit us.'

'Isn't it a bit late for all that now? For playing the dutiful son? For making something of yourself so your mother could be proud of you?' His eyes rose out of the handkerchief.

'Dad, I'm just trying to be true to myself.'

'You mean ...' They were face to face, eye to eye. 'You mean "Take your nose, put it on a lead, and go for a long walk"? Of course, I forgot, I'm just your father.' And a tear swelled over his lower lashes and began its descent down his cheek. Mark found a red paper serviette in his pocket, and with it padded in his fist, stretched out to blot the tear on his father's face. But George got there first, flicking the handkerchief across his cheek before getting up and striding away.

I know we've had our differences, son. We've not always understood each other. But I just hope you'll understand better now the way I've been. Now that you're a father yourself. I cherish the memories of standing with my arms around your mother, watching you asleep in your cot. And the times we drove back from holidays late at night, you in a sleeping bag in the back of the car. I'd lift you out all half asleep and cocooned. I admit, I did think sons were for sweeping the leaves off the drive on a Sunday morning, choosing pretty girlfriends to flatter Dad when they came for tea, following my ambitions. I suppose I just wanted you to do better than me.

But when I hung that charm in the tree with a wish for the little boy, I thought about my own boy too, my extra limb. And I helped myself to a second wish. I can't tell you what it is. Am I allowed a second wish, son? Will it work?

The card that Mark received said:

Dear Mark,

Getting Yvonne's card knocked the legs out from under me. The photo of the three of you in hospital took me back thirty-odd years. Please thank Yvonne for sending it to me. It was good of her. I couldn't address the card to her because I don't know if you two ever did get married. It's none of my business but I wouldn't like to get her surname wrong on the envelope. Anyway it's probably about time I wrote to my own son.

Your news sent me back down memory lane, back to when you were young. Do you remember the wishing tree we used to go to? I went there yesterday. I hung a charm in the tree with a wish for the little boy, and thought about some of the things you and I used to do together. It's a long time, son. Maybe things will be different between us, now that you're a father yourself. I helped myself to a second wish while I was at the tree. I can't tell you what it is of course, but I hope I won't be disappointed.

In exchange for your photo I'm sending one of my house. I built it all with my own hands. It kept me busy after your mother died. I'm proud of it to tell you the truth, and I'd like you to see it sometime.

Best regards,
Dad.

Kith and Kin

Wintry now, Mrs Lipton said to the man who joined the queue at the bus stop.

Sleet flecked his hair and shoulders. She shuffled after the clatter of his words as he turned away, anxious not to waste them. It was impossible to hear what he was saying. But then she saw that he was speaking into a mobile phone. Not to her at all.

Two girls in front of her in the queue looked at their watches. They squinted towards the whiteness at the end of the street.

Two minutes late, one said to the other. They stamped their feet. Shit.

Their vigil reminded her of the knicker-wetting tension of being 'it' when she was a child playing 'Turn-the-wheel tig'. You couldn't start chasing the others until the first vehicle came around the corner. Sometimes she seemed to hold her breath for ever. There weren't too many vehicles then. Nowadays she'd taken up a kind of 'hospital tig'. You had to clutch the part of you that had been tigged, as if you were wounded. Ankle, shoulder, behind. These days she was clutching her hips, where age had caught them. But there wasn't really anyone to chase. Just as well.

It's coming. I'll catch you later, said the man, turning back to face her. Yup, yup, cheers.

Mrs Lipton felt his impatience shoving her from behind as she persuaded her feet up the high steps. What she really needed, as ever, was a supportive hand. Though someone nice to have a chatter with would have been welcome too. She reached forward for the rail – awkward, with her stick in one hand and the fist of coins in the other, ready in case she needed cash as well as her pass. She became a foreigner trying to interpret the way to do things.

You've raised those steps since the last time, she joked to the driver. Gave my new hip quite a stretch.

On you go, he said, glancing at her pass.

She used the stick as a tripod to stabilize her as she moved down the lurching bus. There was a hothouse atmosphere. Steamed up windows stopped the passengers seeing fully the world they'd come from. They could end up in quite another one. In Timbuktu or somewhere. She lowered herself into the first empty seat, back to the driver. It was a relief to sit down. Her hips were a damn nuisance, but she relished the link to royalty they gave her. She'd broken one at the same time as the Queen Mother. Exactly the same time.

Funny that. Both back on our pins thanks to modern technology. And those lovely nurses.

The mobile man glanced at her from diagonally opposite. She smiled, happier with him now that she was settled. There were a few familiar faces – Mrs Ansell waved from a few rows back. Mrs Lipton nodded to Mrs Carroll across the aisle as she arranged her gloves in her lap and wedged the stick so as not to trip anyone.

How are you?

Keeping well, Mrs Carroll. Yes.

Shopping is it?

She nodded. Nodding an untruth wasn't really the same as speaking one. She could have just been flicking the drips out of her eyes. What would they think if she admitted she was just there for the ride, for old time's sake. While she still could. The bag clasped in front of her could easily have contained a long list of things to buy and carry home, and a packet of blackcurrant pastilles – the ones she used to suck as she bussed into town every Monday. The ones she had to remember not to chew because they snarled up her dentures.

But finding Ponds Vanishing Cream on the shelves in Boots had long ago become an assault course of heavy doors and escalators, even before she had to confront shelves of identical products. Why did they have to make it so difficult? She didn't go shopping in town any more. A weekly box of groceries was brought to her door. Same every week. Except sometimes it was malt loaf rather than lemon Madeira. She wasn't sure why. Maybe lemons were out of season. She had to put the malt loaf out for the birds anyway. It was too sticky for her.

She opened her hand and looked at the coins that she hadn't needed in the end. Even after all this time, they looked unfamiliar. Was it with Sheila, or Sheila's mother she'd watched *Blue Peter* a few years ago? They'd been burying a time capsule in the BBC grounds. It was that tall chap, Peter Pervert, in flared trousers and the long hair that seemed to be in fashion these days. They'd just turned the money decimal and buried a set of the new coins in the time capsule. Could have buried the whole blasted lot as far as she was concerned. It had been confusing, and still was, trying to convert prices back to shillings to know what they were worth.

I saw Mrs Everett yesterday, Mrs Carroll said.

Oh yes, said Mrs Lipton.

She looked lovely. In a blue dress. Fitted her like a glove.

Mrs Lipton's eyes settled on the face opposite her. A girl, dark, a scarf wrapped over her. You could see the layers of it, wrapping and re-wrapping around her head and neck like a cocoon.

The man with the phone was brushing steam away from a small patch of window with his springy hair. Through the gap he created, she saw grey sleet-filled sky, tree tops and lit-up windows in the flats and houses they passed, peering into the bus from above.

The face opposite was very dark. African. You saw them in the town sometimes these days, like those rare tropical birds you heard about blowing off course and hiding from thousands of bird-watchers in gorse bushes in Cornwall. Being one on your own must be hard, she thought. Like being her age alone among a party of Sheila's generation.

When she was young they hadn't seen the dark ones really. There were Italians, who were what they called 'olive-skinned', and an Egyptian man they used to gawp at while he danced for money outside the picture hall. During World War I, a party of Canadian Indian troops had swept through town and they were coffee-coloured.

What was his name – the commander? Chief Clear Sky. That was it. Funny really, his name, seeing as how we treated them to all that drizzle. And some of them ended up with the flu. Or so mother told me. She's very dark, that one.

The girl opposite smiled at Mrs Lipton.

•   •   •   •   •   •   •   •   •   •   •   •   •   •   •   •   •

Rehema could sense the old lady's acquaintances tied loosely throughout the rows and aisles of the bus like the knots in a fishing net. It reminded her of home – how you knew people. She did her level best to cast a hook deep and pull out a smile. She wondered where the old lady was going, and why she talked to herself every now and again and twitched when she looked at her watch.

Age made her think of her father. What would he make of her life here? How was he going to choose the winner of the challenge he had set the three of them when their mother died and he had retired to bed? You have to make something of yourselves, he'd said. Return to me when you have done it. Tell me your successes, then I'll tell you what you have won.

She was the last-born and the first to leave, on a scholarship. She shouldered the aspirations of the whole village; played out all their ideas about leaving the island, or going to Europe just to see what was there. To see if it was true, what some of the youngsters had learned from films in town, that there were streets full of cars and rich people. That there was a better life.

What would she tell her father of her successes?

She had almost learned to bear the cold. She would return home at the end of the year with a refrigerator for the family home. A fitting memento. She would have learned European ways and have white friends. A shoal of whispers would wash through the village from behind once familiar hands, bending and yielding like sea ferns. The 'been to' bringing home the promise of sophistication and possessions.

How would her achievements compare to her brother, the first-born, who had gone to the town and taken a job as a waiter? These days he seemed to like the ways of the tourists who took off their clothes to burn in the sun. He went to the gardens every evening to talk English with them. He had already saved enough to buy a bicycle. Perhaps he'd put a white wife on the back of it and cycle across the island to show her to father. His success.

How would her achievements compare to her brother, the second-born, who had refused to leave? By day, he fished from the same boats that Father had. By night he looked after the old man. He wouldn't have a refrigerator or an *mzungu* wife to show. He wouldn't experience shops and TVs and telephones and reliable water supplies. He could hardly win Father's prize.

She pictured his evenings – the same old thing. The *hodi-hodi* call would alert him to visitors who took shape out of the night. He'd call back *karibu* welcoming them to sit and talk on the front step, go into the lamplight to pay respects to Father. As they talked, a chorus of waves would pour across the beach and the wind shiver the palms. She heard the hollow knock of seeds on the wooden pockets of the *Bao* board. And there was something else – laughter – ringing across the night. He had allowed himself to be left behind, caught up in old ways, but at least it meant Father was cared for.

She looked out at the day, sliced open and defined by the crescent sweep of the windscreen wipers. Nine o'clock in the morning and it was still making up its mind whether or not to get light. This greyness had been skulking around for the last hour. She lived in fear that one day it would decide not to bother to turn into a day. Yesterday she'd wanted to chide the lazy sun. Even though the sky was clear as she'd walked the Sunday city to find where the people were, the sun hadn't penetrated some of the streets. It had left frost casing cars and pavements all day. Even at noon it barely skimmed the skyline, just turning golden the tips of the chimney pots on the highest buildings. It had none of the impertinence of an equatorial sunrise that happened in a chink of time between night and day. Where the sun leapt perpendicular into the sky from a flat sea and pulled everyone out of their beds with it. It began to burn and bite them from high overhead by seven in the morning. Here at least there was no need to hide from the sun.

These days she woke cautiously, conspiring with the bed covers that entangled her. In her first lecture each morning, she still felt she was awakening from hibernation, or a sleep of fairy-tale length. She felt the blood beginning to reach into feet frozen from the bus journey, feet that thawed into a hot itch. Her eyelids drooped. She had to fight the tide which washed her back towards her bed, the place she retreated to by eight every evening, relieved by the weight of covers over her head.

She had suspected an illness. Her joints were filled with daily pains and she would have been called *mzungu* if they saw her at home now, she was so pale. But it was just the cold monster nibbling at her. It was part and parcel of learning new ways and making discoveries about this place. She was acclimatizing. That's what she told Father in her letters home.

A stray thought sprang up and slapped her cheek. Father might die while she was away from home. How could she win his prize then?

She set her jaw against the icy blast which swept damp students and nurses into the bus. As they passed, they radiated coldness and the echoes of tunes they shared from their headphones. She didn't smile at them or wish them good morning, even the ones she saw every day. She understood now that this made you seem simple. Even smiles and greetings wouldn't do, let alone the friendly slap of hands she would expect at home. She felt she had packed away a part of herself for the whole year she would spend here. It was important in order to fit in.

One of the old lady's gloves slid across her lap and onto the floor.

Sorry, madam, she said. Your glove.

● ● ● ● ● ● ● ● ● ● ● ● ● ● ● ●

Thank you dear. I'd have missed that when I got off. Mrs Lipton nodded at the window. It's wintry now.

It is.

The girl had a nice smile, white teeth against black skin.

She's probably about the same age as Sheila. In her twenties. Twenty-something.

Twenty nine, the dark girl said to her.

Had she said it out loud then? Age making her ridiculous. Rude, even. She looked at her watch to cover her embarrassment.

Will you still be on time? The girl asked.

Mrs Lipton smiled, destinations and times too slippery to recall just now. She leant forward towards the girl. They'd been talking about the twenties, hadn't they? They'd been having quite a chat.

I grew up then you know. The 'Roaring Twenties' we called them. Such a time.

Is it?

Everything happened then.

Everything?

We got the first movies, trams came to town, some people even got electric and gas. And the music. She smacked her lips a couple of times then gazed upwards and wavered a few words in song. 'I'll always be in love with you. I'll never ...' dum de dum. It was wonderful.

She sat back again. That was before they knew there was going to be another war, she thought.

Wars with gaps. My life has been pretty much just wars with gaps.

There are no wars these days, mm?

Mrs Lipton craned her neck around to see where they were but was distracted by an advertisement hoarding on which a naked woman sprawled next to an outsize jar of coffee. She held egg-timers to her breasts. 'Grab the instant ...' it read, '... and keep abreast of life'. She stared until it faded into a blur of rain. Everyone was fixated with sex nowadays.

Do you know, my son-in-law found a pike in a telephone box.

A pike – what is it?

A kind of fish.

Ah, thank you. I try to understand each and every thing about English, but there are too many words. She smiled and then frowned. It was a fish. In a telephone box?

Yes, dear. Its gills were still flapping. It didn't revive when he took it home and put it in the bath, either.

She looked at her watch again, trying to remember why she had started to tell the girl this story. These days she was like a pike in a telephone box herself. That was it.

Really, when you got to her age, your body just hung on you like an old overcoat. A wet and heavy overcoat that you were forced to wear through a hot summer. You longed to shrug it off. What was there to look forward to? She waited for a smudge of something in her mind to refine into a pearl. Apart from seeing the new baby – of course.

She'd read somewhere recently that scientists in the next century would be able to keep people alive to the age of a hundred and thirty. But who would want to live that long? Where would they put everyone while they lived out their vegetable years? Maybe they'd stack them up in multi-storey capsules like those Japanese hotels Sheila had talked about. If attached to drips and catheters they could be pretty much ignored for a few years she supposed. Then die of natural causes. They'd vanish from public life, like the 'disappeared' in those Latin countries. Did they have 'the disappeared' in Africa too she wondered. Maybe she could ask the girl.

Her family certainly wouldn't want her to live to a hundred and thirty. They were troubled enough about her now. She used to keep track of the days going past by the build up of dust on the sideboard. But they'd taken this natural clock away by employing a cleaner. It had confused her. Her hair kept her right though. She could keep track of her permanent growing out in the mirror. And the fortnightly visits from the hairdresser kept her in touch with the roll of the months around the year.

They'll put me into a home, you know.

The girl nodded but Mrs Lipton didn't think she'd caught her meaning.

They don't think I can manage an evening meal for myself. From the freezer to the oven. I'll forget what I'm doing half way through. Put it from the oven back into the freezer instead of into myself.

The girl laughed.

And wonder why I feel hungry and the freezer's defrosting.

They laughed together. Mrs Lipton was on a run now.

Or maybe they're afraid I'll put it straight into myself, bypassing the oven. And wonder why my dentures aren't up to it. She opened her mouth and pushed her dentures forward, waggling them to illustrate the meaning of the word.

The girl's laugh was loud enough that it stirred mobile man from his slump against the window.

Shall I get off at Paul Street or George Street? He asked his phone.

Mrs Lipton took a few blinks to register the meaning of his words, and that they weren't intended to add to the conversation.

They've made people like that. Have to consult someone about every little thing.

The bus rattled at a junction. They must be getting close to the centre. She swivelled stiffly in her seat to look through the windscreen. She saw that they were only at the clock tower roundabout and heard the chimes go for nine over the bus engine. Each peal reassured her. The bus had caught up with the timetable, despite its late start. They would all be on time.

But then she realized. She had no appointment, no particular reason to get off anywhere. Anytime.

It's running on time, she said to the dark girl as she eased herself back around.

• • • • • • • • • • • • • • • • •

Rehema felt the sway of the intermittent wipers. Swish-swish. She felt they were in league with the rhythm of the clock-face illuminated below a pointed spire. Tick-tock. It was like an eye. The face blinked clear then gradually blurred by slushy water. Blink. Clear to opaque. The chimes rang out for nine o'clock, addressing the bus passengers like a strict teacher with a whip.

Ah, so it's on time. She nodded.

She heard bells from her bedsit room too, thin and metallic in the cold air. On the hour. All day and all night. They were followed by silence, or sometimes by traffic noises on the street. When she'd first arrived the chimes woke her every hour through the night. She climbed out of bed and stood at the window, pulled back the curtains to see what it was telling people to do. But she saw no special response.

The *muezzin's* call to prayer at dawn stretched open-throated in her memory. She recalled the way it circled the village, echoing in the narrow gaps between houses, squeezing through open casements, wafting the gauze of mosquito nets onto limbs. It tugged at their hands as they drowsed off the sides of beds, pulling the men to the mosque, the women to their prayer mats and then to their stoves to cook breakfast. The burning charcoal tickled their nostrils awake. At home the days were portioned out by the lines of men's heads bobbing up and down in the gloom of the mosque; disembodied white caps glimpsed through open doorways. And the sails of *dhows*, tipped crazily on the horizon, going out and coming back in from the fishing.

But here the bells seemed to talk to themselves, just told people whether or not they were on time. A one-eyed god who watched over them. These days she had almost stopped hearing them.

Streets as busy as ever, the old lady said. All that noise.

Rehema thought about the streets. Sometimes she walked to the university, first putting the bus fare into a jar labelled 'refrigerator'. She walked and walked and walked, wearing layers of clothes she had to unpeel later, like an onion. The colours she saw were so polite compared to the turquoises and reds and rich skin browns of home. She passed signs outside cafes that said 'Good News for Cold people ... Hot chocolate, Cappuccino ...' You had to pay one pound a cup for it. She thought of the man in her village who sold her coconuts to drink, cool from the back of his bicycle. He just charged her a few shillings and usually gave her a free one to take to her father. They were relatives in some undefined way.

Walking home along her street in the evening, she saw into brightly lit rooms where families gathered around a TV, or sat at computers, or ate around a table set with flowers. Their homes looked so beautiful. She was a little sad that nothing of their lives penetrated the glass. She longed to smell their food. Would garlic and ginger and cardamom have thawed her senses? They spoke without sound. There was no way to stop in passing to exchange news of the day, she could only wave through their windows. But they didn't seem to see. She wasn't in the light for them, like they were for her. She wondered if she would ever see the inside of a Scottish home. If anyone would invite her.

She listed in her head what streets were made of. They were people, wheels and buildings, wherever you were. But these streets had timetables too. They were so efficient. People did not like to wait. She supposed it was because it became boring, if you didn't like to talk much either. The old lady seemed to like to talk, she was so friendly, but Rehema wasn't always sure who she was talking to.

Actually, Rehema said. In my country, we are only happy if there is noise. We like too much to have noise on the bus. I find it is very nice here – the quiet. Very nice.

What sort of noise?

Okay. We have music playing, people laughing, boys calling out to friends and neighbours we pass.

Oh, I see dear.

And we have a conductor. When it's very full, he hangs onto the back of the bus. It's dangerous. You hear him, chipping a coin to tell the driver when to stop. She used her knuckles rat-a-tat-tat against the book she held in her lap and then looked down at it, suddenly quiet.

She had felt for a moment the rush of hot air and sand through the open sides of a bus. It stuck into the crevices of skin and hair and sent hands to bat at the swirling dances of loose clothing.

•   •   •   •   •   •   •   •   •   •   •   •   •   •   •   •

See you outside Debenhams, mobile man said. Cheers.

Just like going to the doctor, Mrs Lipton said.

Yes?

I don't like telephones, you know.

They'd always made her nervous – afraid to take too long, afraid to make a call that wasn't for an arrangement of some sort. They hadn't needed them when she was young. They just went to each other's doors.

These days you have to have an appointment even to see your own family. Do you know, when I was a child, we were marched off to visit aunts and grannies every Sunday. After church. We weren't given a choice.

The dark girl laughed.

My granddaughter, Sheila, had her second baby last week.

Ah, this means a grand … no, *great* grandchild. Is it boy or girl?

A girl.

She looked at the streets outside through the steamed up windows, thought about the little princess she hadn't seen yet. When would Sheila bring her, she wondered? Would she ever?

I'm going to visit her, she said. Today. She lives on the other side of town.

Mrs Lipton surprised herself. She didn't know this had been her intention. Or had she just forgotten? The doors hissed open and a stream of people made for the door. It must be the High Street. The mobile man stood up.

Goodbye, Mrs Lipton said. But he only frowned at her stick as he caught it slightly with his foot.

We're at the shops, dear. Mrs Carroll offered her a gap in which to get up and join the flow.

I'm not going shopping. I'm visiting Sheila. She has a new baby, you know.

Ooh, how lovely. Don't you want to do your shopping first?

No, thank you. She looked straight ahead, avoiding Mrs Carroll's eyes. Mrs Carroll moved up the bus towards the door.

Mrs Lipton looked straight into the black eyes opposite her. Perhaps the girl would like to visit Sheila with her. She might not have ever seen a white baby. If she worked at the hospital, she'd get off the next stop. If she was a student at the university it would be the one after that.

You're nearly there are you dear?

Yes?

Your stop. Is it the next one?

Actually, I'm going to the university, the dark girl said. I'm studying.

Clever girl. Just like Sheila. Two stops then.

And is it the same stop for you, madam?

After yours dear. Three stops more.

Mrs Lipton renewed with a glove the clearer patch on the window that mobile man had made. Sleet was lying in slushy puddles. It would be slippery. Why hadn't she just stayed at home? Sheila might not even be in. You should have rung me, she'd say. We could have arranged a time, Granny. No point in you braving Siberia at your age. We could just have a chat on the phone.

If she stayed on, the bus would take her in a big loop, back home. There wouldn't be any need for hobbling up and down bus steps or slipping along icy pavements. With her hips, it would be safer. But she did want to see the baby. Her first great-granddaughter. And she certainly wouldn't be making many more trips like this before she was packed off.

The bus stopped for the hospital and the nurses padded off in their neat black shoes. The dark girl remained. They were left more alone as the bus growled towards the periphery of town. Without the touchstone of the other passengers, they both relaxed.

My name is Rehema.

Sorry?

Rehema.

I see. Mine is ... What should the girl call her? A

first name would be over-familiar. What would be right? I know. Call me Granny.

Granny, the girl repeated with a smile.

Yes. Just like Sheila does. Mrs Lipton leant forwards. You know, I'm a great-granny now.

Rehema continued to smile.

It would be nice to have some company when she went to see Sheila and the wee girl, Mrs Lipton thought.

• • • • • • • • • • • • • • • • • •

Rehema anticipated for Granny the welcome of a room with flowers. She would soon be on the inside of the glass. With her granddaughter. And great-granddaughter. Even so, she worried a little about the old lady getting there alone, without a friendly arm to dovetail under hers. She seemed to have such difficulty in walking. At home she would have stayed on the bus to help the lady off, even walked her to the family house.

She imagined returning to Father with not just a refrigerator, but photographs of Granny with a baby on her lap. The old lady could be her first *mzungu* friend. She'd like to be part of Granny's web. That would really be making something of herself. Once home she could write letters to an address in Glasgow while she rested on the porch in the evenings. She imagined the older village women gathering around and laughing as Rehema translated the stories in the old lady's letters.

But she couldn't offer to help Granny. The old lady would think something bad about her. She had learned that people didn't like you to be too friendly. They liked to be alone sometimes. She would have to return to Father with a different story. She thought how she would like to return to him now, even without a success to show him, to feel the sun burning her skin again and join in the laughter of her family.

The bus started to slow down and students trailed

long wet trousers and tinny musical beats to the front. Rehema stood to join them.

I am very happy to meet you, she said to Mrs Lipton. I have to get off now.

Lovely to meet you too. Take care. It's wintry now.

It is, said the girl. Goodbye, Granny. Saying the name made her think of Annie, one of her fellow students. But this was the first time she'd come across the name 'Granny'. She placed a hand on Mrs Lipton's shoulder as she walked past her. It was snatched away as she tripped into a run to keep her balance when the bus shuddered to a halt. As she stepped out of the bus, she embraced herself more tightly in the loops of scarf around her head to keep out the chill.

• • • • • • • • • • • • • • • • • •

She was a nice girl, Mrs Lipton thought. Like Sheila. They'd get on. Did she tell me her name? It's a shame she's not coming with me. What was the reason now?

Sheila would be tickled if she introduced her to a darkie. You'll get yourself into trouble, Sheila always told her, talking to all these strangers. This is nearly the twenty-first century, Granny. It's not safe. But then most of them didn't talk back.

As the bus pulled away, Mrs Lipton could just see the smudged outline of a figure on the pavement. It looked wide, puffed up with layers of clothes. A blurred arm rose up from it, like someone casting a fishing line. It was a wave. Probably intended for her.

Her hand fluttered up a little from her lap, like a butterfly abandoned on a windowsill by the retreat of summer. Now she felt tired. She felt like a little lie down and a listen to the morning story. Where had she been intending to go anyway? She let the bus carry her on along its route, around the loop. It was too much effort to think about doing anything else. She'd done quite enough sightseeing.

As the bus splashed along Sheila's road, she brushed back the drips of condensation from the window and tried to pick out the house in the terrace. Her eyes snatched at a brightly lit front-room window. But they passed too quickly to see who was inside, to catch sight of her little princess. Her hand fluttered up briefly a second time, but it was obvious that there was no one to see her wave.

11:9 Publishing October 2000

The Wolfclaw Chronicles
Tom Bryan
A powerful debut novel bridging the cultures of Ireland,
Russia, Canada, Scotland and England.
ISBN 1-903238-10-2
Price £9.99

Rousseau Moon
David Cameron
Lyrical, intense, sensitive, foreboding – a remarkable first
collection.
ISBN 1-903238-15-3
Price £9.99

Life Drawing
Linda Cracknell
The eagerly awaited first collection from an award-
winning writer.
ISBN 1-903238-13-7
Price £9.99

Hi Bonnybrig & Other Greetings
Shug Hanlan
Strikingly original short stories and a very funny novella.
ISBN 1-903238-16-1
Price £9.99

The Tin Man
Martin Shannon
A debut novel from a new and exciting young writer.
ISBN 1-903238-11-0
Price £9.99

Occasional Demons
Raymond Soltysek
A dark, menacing and quite dazzling collection from one
of Scotland's most talented new writers.
ISBN 1-903238-12-9
Price £9.99

About 11:9

Who makes the decisions?

11:9 titles are selected by an editorial board of six people: Douglas Gifford, Professor and Head of Department of Scottish Literature, University of Glasgow; Donny O'Rourke, poet, lecturer and journalist; Paul Pender, screenwriter and independent film producer; Jan Rutherford, specialist in book marketing and promotion; Marion Sinclair, former editorial director of Polygon and lecturer in publishing and Neil Wilson, managing director of 11:9.

Our aims

Supported by the Scottish Arts Council National Lottery Fund and partnership funding, 11:9 publish the work of writers both unknown and established, living and working in Scotland or from a Scottish background.
11:9's brief is to publish contemporary literary novels, and is actively searching for new talent. If you wish to submit work send an introductory letter, a brief synopsis of your novel, a biographical note about yourself and two typed sample chapters to: Editorial Administrator, 11:9, Neil Wilson Publishing Ltd, Suite 303a, The Pentagon Centre, 36 Washington Street, Glasgow, G3 8AZ. Details are also available from our website at **www.11-9.co.uk.**

If you would like to be added to a mailing list about future publications, either register on our website or send your name and address to 11:9, Neil Wilson Publishing Ltd, Suite 303a, The Pentagon Centre, 36 Washington Street, Glasgow, G3 8AZ.

11:9 refers to 11 September 1997 when the Scottish people voted to re-establish their parliament in Edinburgh.